Escaping the Emotional Roller Coaster

Dr. Patricia E. Zurita Ona, or Dr. Z., is a clinical psychologist who specializes in OCD, trauma, all types of anxiety and related conditions, and emotion dysregulation problems for children, teens, and adults. She's the director and founder of the East Bay Behavior Therapy Center, a private therapy center in Walnut Creek, California. In addition to private practice, Dr. Z. is a clinical faculty member for the Wright Institute, and regularly attends both national and international conferences.

Escaping the Emotional Roller Coaster

ACT for the EMOTIONALLY SENSITIVE

Dr. Patricia Zurita Ona

"Having intense emotions makes it difficult to act effectively in the moment. Dr. Z. offers a vast array of practical tools and strategies to achieve a life worth living even with these roller-coaster emotions."

— Christophe Deval, M.S.C., therapist, talent development director at KPMG in Paris, France, and author of *Découvrir l'ACT , Simplifiez vos relations avec les autres*, and *Vous avez tout pour réussir*

"Zurita Ona provides a veritable treasure chest of strategies you can use to make your emotions work for you, rather than against you. It isn't a bad thing to be a 'super-feeler', it is a good thing! I highly recommend this wonderful step by step program to help you develop a new level of emotional intelligence!"

— Kirk Strosahl Ph.D., author of *The Mindfulness and Acceptance Workbook for Depression: Using Acceptance and Commitment Therapy to move through depression and live a life worth living*

"Rarely, have I read a book that has provided me with true insights as to how one thinks, feels as a super-feeler and what to do about it. Reading Dr. Z.'s book gave me hope. If you read her book, you know that you are not alone and that there is help for you."

— Susan Gurley, Executive Director of the Anxiety and Depression Association of America (ADAA)

"Dr. Z. takes a refreshing long-term approach of self-discovery and self-mastery to help people escape their emotional 'do-loop' and move forward in life. Effectively balancing the science of emotional behavior with simple practical approaches, she helps us understand our 'emotional machinery', build core coping skills, and shift from 'I feel, therefore I act' to 'I feel, therefore I am'."

— Charles Calderaro, Senior Vice President of Global Manufacturing for a biotechnology company focused on rare diseases

"This hopeful book, using scores of examples, provides an action-oriented approach for achieving strategies to deal with difficult emotions effectively . . . you will acquire skills and tools to live a life based on your own values and improve connections with the people you love."

— Leslie Elliott, strong advocate for mental health services and the removal of stigma related to it

First published 2018

Exisle Publishing Pty Ltd
PO Box 864, Chatswood, NSW 2057, Australia
226 High Street, Dunedin, 9016, New Zealand
www.exislepublishing.com

A CiP record for this book is available from the National Library of Australia.

ISBN 978-1-925335-74-3

Designed by Nick Turzynski, redinc. Book Design
Typeset in Source Sans Pro 12/16
Printed in China

This book uses paper sourced under ISO 14001 guidelines from well-managed forests and other controlled sources.

10 9 8 7 6 5 4 3 2 1

Disclaimer

While this book is intended as a general information resource and all care has been taken in compiling the contents, neither the author nor the publisher and their distributors can be held responsible for any loss, claim or action that may arise from reliance on the information contained in this book. As each person and situation is unique, it is the responsibility of the reader to consult a qualified professional regarding their personal care.

This book is dedicated to all the super-feelers I have worked with. You're not broken and you're not alone; you're just wired to feel a lot.

Contents

Introduction

At one point or another, we all have been dragged by our emotions, up and down, left and right, and in all directions; the challenge is that in this moment, there are approximately 20 million Americans struggling with emotion regulation on a daily basis — not just from time to time, but almost all the time. I call them super-feelers.

This book is written for the super-feelers, thinking of you, your daily struggles, and what you experience in your life; when you read it, you will see that these pages tap into core challenges super-feelers face. Instead of putting on Band-Aids that only work temporarily, it's about showing you, step-by-step, behaviorally speaking, how to stop living in agony because of all the emotional noise you go through.

The skills presented in these chapters are based on an empirically supported approach called Acceptance and Commitment Therapy (ACT), and incorporate current findings of emotion science, neurobiology of attachment, and affective neuroscience.

As a therapist who sees clients on a daily basis, I can tell you that writing this book was a highlight of my year, because:

■ I studied affective science from the work of Dr. Antonio Damasio (1994) through Dr. Lisa Feldman Barrett (2017) and everything in between.

- I bored my friends with nerdy comments about different modes of emotion regulation.
- I indulged myself with the words of Dr. Dan Siegel and the neurobiology of attachment.
- I dug into the work of Dr. Richard Davidson, who has studied for years our emotional landscape in the brain.
- I reviewed all clinical applications from different therapy modalities in the work of super-feelers.
- I tortured my students with presenting this book and the ideas behind it.

There are so many things that are out of our control in life: natural disasters, car crashes, people leaving town, our bodies aging. And even when we think we have everything under control, life brings new, totally unexpected circumstances. We don't have control of what happens around us or how we quickly feel about those events, but we can *choose* how to respond to those overwhelming, distressful and uncomfortable feelings we go through when things go wrong. This book is about teaching super-feelers how to *choose* their responses when their emotional machinery gets turned on and attempts to drive their behavior.

I deeply believe that super-feelers deserve an amazing life, and an amazing life is the one they *choose* to live from moment to moment. Not the one that their emotional machinery chooses for them.

I hope you find this book helpful, enjoy reading it, and practice the skills you will learn on a daily basis. Bon voyage!

Warmly,

Dr. Z.
Patricia E. Zurita Ona, Psy.D.

SECTION 1

Life as a
Super-Feeler

Chapter 1: Am I a Super-Feeler?

- Have you been told you are too sensitive or that everything is a big emotional deal for you?
- Do you sometimes feel overwhelmed by your emotions — like a knob turned all the way up for anger, anxiety, guilt, sadness, and other emotions?
- Do you experience your emotions so intensely, as being overpowering, that you cannot manage your behavior or think clearly in the moment?
- Do you regret how you behave because in a given moment you do exactly what you feel?
- Are you exhausted from going up and down, left and right, because of overwhelming emotions?

If you answered yes to any of these questions, chances are you are a super-feeler.

Everyone, at one point or another, feels overwhelmed with crushing emotions and doesn't know how to handle them. Super-feelers, however, feel their emotions as if they have a switch that turns on and off — they feel too much, too quickly, and they act too soon, as if they're being kicked, stomped on, and knocked down to the floor by those feelings. (Be aware that throughout this book, the terms *emotions* and *feelings* are used interchangeably. Also, to avoid confusion, let's distinguish emotions or feelings from moods: *mood* is a long-lasting state, while an emotion or a feeling is a transitory experience.)

If you're a super-feeler, your emotions are running your behaviors, 24/7, with no vacations and no holidays. For instance, when you feel guilty, you're pulverized with guilt; when you feel anxious, you're crushed with anxiety; when you feel sad, you're flooded with sadness. You experience your emotions quickly and intensely; believe every thought, interpretation, or hypothesis that comes into your mind as if it were the absolute truth; and then do exactly what the emotion tells you to do. Later on, you regret your actions because you get hurt and the people you care about get hurt, too.

Going through this dance with your emotions, up and down, left and right, back and forth, is exhausting, and you find your life is full of broken relationships, loneliness, difficulties holding a job, and perhaps, even suicidal thoughts. It's not easy for you, and it's not easy for the people around you.

As a super-feeler, you're dealing with emotion regulation problems — as all people do at times — but because of your makeup, you feel most of your emotions at a maximum level, turned all the way up, and despite your efforts, you frequently get stuck on a reactive chain of emotion after emotion, almost on a daily basis. You may wonder . . .

How Did I Become a Super-Feeler?

On the day of my thirty-fifth birthday, my boyfriend and I were hosting a party together. This relationship was my fifth attempt to create a family life with someone I love. I met him through an online dating website, and after dating for eight months, I felt that he was the one. We argued a lot, sometimes for hours, days, and even weeks, but I still believed he was the one.

On the day of my birthday, I was really upset with him because he wasn't helping me as much as I wanted him to. I got so mad that I started yelling at him, calling him names, complaining about how he never helps me, how he's a slob, and cannot seem to keep up with me, even for such an easy task as putting together a party. I was so angry that I took off for an hour to the coffee shop next door and sat there crying, texting him, still angry. When I got back to the apartment, my boyfriend was gone, and his most important belongings were gone, too. There was a piece of paper on the hardwood floor: 'For eight months I asked you to pay attention to your anger, the way you treat me when you get angry, and even when I'm here with you with all my love, you cannot do it. I'm scared and cannot do this to myself. I'm out of this relationship; I'm done.'
— A SUPER-FEELER

Have you been in Stacey's shoes? Despite her desire to have a family life, her emotions dictated her actions 24/7 in the relationship with her boyfriend, and she ended up with a fifth breakup. Why does this keep happening to her? What makes her get so angry at her boyfriend so quickly and so often?

Here is a three-part response to make sense of Stacey's behavior: 1) her temperament, 2) her limbic system, and 3) her learning history.

YOUR TEMPERAMENT

Your genetic makeup predisposes you to a particular type of emotional baseline from which you respond to your internal and external world;

we call this "temperament." Some people are wired to be sharpeners and others are levelers. Levelers are usually more mellow-yellow, as my students once said, and it takes a lot for them to have a reaction. Sharpeners, on the other hand, tend to be more sensitive, attuned, and impressionable; they react more to their surroundings, people's facial expressions and tone of voice, noise, sensory stimuli, and so on.

Super-feelers tend to have a sharpener temperament in general.

YOUR LIMBIC SYSTEM

The limbic system is the area of the brain in charge of emotional processing, and it has a set of structures that interact together. There are two organs that play a key role: the amygdala and the hippocampus.

The amygdala, even though it is about the size of an almond, has the incredible power to alert us when a situation is perceived as threatening, signaling a "danger alarm" in our brain and compelling us to take immediate action. The hippocampus stores the specifics of a situation, including the dry facts, and basically acts as the memory of the limbic system. The amygdala and the hippocampus together, as safety guards, check whether a current situation matches or is similar to an alarming past encounter, and if the match is positive, then the amygdala signals the danger alarm. It's as if your body hears a fire alarm or a car honking at you when you're crossing the street.

The challenge with the interaction between the hippocampus and the amygdala is that, given the hundreds of experiences you go through on any given day, most of the time there are pieces of data, situations, and events in the present that are connected to past encounters that have been perceived as uncomfortable, risky, or threatening. Because of this association between the past and the present, the fire alarm of your limbic system gets activated over and over again, even if you're not in danger at that moment.

Different neurological studies have suggested that super-feelers have an overactive amygdala, which explains why they often exhibit a higher frequency of emotional and behavioral reactivity across various situations; super-feelers, in a nutshell, are biologically predisposed to feel too much, too quickly, and to behave reactively in the moment.

YOUR LEARNING HISTORY

Did you ever attend a class called Emotions 101? Of course not. We learn as we go. Since you were born, you've been learning through every single encounter you have in your life. As a baby, you learned about the world through your senses; it's a sensory world based on what you see, hear, touch, taste, and smell. When you learn to talk, you continue learning through the use of language and by making all types of associations, relationships, and connections in a symbolic world: words, sentences, memories, and so on. You're constantly learning, every moment, without end. Sometimes you learn information by explicitly being told or taught or by searching yourself; other times, you're just exposed to information that you're not even fully aware of. Can you imagine in this moment all the information you have in your brain, things that you know you know and all the things that you don't know you know?

As a super-feeler, you learned to handle your emotional landscape based on all the direct and indirect memos you received from the people around you, from the different relationships you participated in, and from all the societal messages about the "right" way to handle emotions; it's your learning history.

For instance, Stacey recalled different memories when she was 11 years old in which every time her brother was playing with her favorite toys, or her mom refused to give her dessert, or her father didn't want to take her to swim, she felt outrage and then screamed from the bottom of her lungs at everyone until they gave up and responded to her needs. In Stacey's words, she didn't know what else to do to get what she needed at times because she felt that nobody listened to her as the baby daughter. Stacey learned to deal with intense anger and other emotions as best she could, and this became part of her learning history. Later on, because she couldn't tolerate the intensity and stress that came with feeling angry, hurt, or disappointed, she sometimes used drugs, cut her wrists, or tried to make sense of her struggle by blaming others.

It's the interaction among your temperament, limbic system, and learning history that creates your personal signature as a super-feeler.

It's Courageous to Be in Your Shoes

It's really hard to go through the swing of emotions up and down, left and right, and up and down again when your emotional switch is on, dragging you into emotional hell, and your limbic system is working really hard to get your attention, organizing your body around a particular action-urge, and demanding you do something right away. It's tough — really tough.

Nobody knows what happens under your skin when your emotional machinery gets activated and all the effort it takes you to not do whatever those distressing and obnoxious feelings tell you to do. It's actually courageous to be in your shoes and to handle your feelings, given how little latitude your amygdala provides in any particular moment. Many super-feelers, in an attempt to manage their intense emotions, rely on unconstructive responses. I call these "quick fixes," because they might work in the short term, but they get you into even more trouble in the long run. These unhelpful — even risky — responses are the subject of the next chapter.

Chapter 2: Why Your Quick Fixes Aren't Working

When your emotional machinery gets activated, you go from one feeling to another, like an emotional chain, and if some of those feelings are uncomfortable, like any human being, you will naturally do whatever it takes to suppress, minimize, or neutralize your discomfort right away. We all do things that pay off immediately, especially when we are distressed; it's as if getting an offer today of $100 for a talk is more attractive than an offer of $150 next week for the same talk.

Trying to Manage Feelings with Quick Fixes

Super-feelers, with their best efforts and intentions, do what they can to manage their crushing emotions, and sometimes they manage them with quick fixes. Let's briefly look at each one.

SCOTCH, SEX, WORK, AND CHOCOLATE

> *It's 11:00 p.m. Monday night, and after having a long day at work, Jeff, a super-feeler, arrives home ready to*

eat. There is Bob, waiting for him, and after greeting him, Bob says, "Why didn't you reply to my text this afternoon?" Jeff quickly looks at him, and even though he is tired, he stares angrily at Bob and screams, "Is this how you greet me on a Monday night at 11 p.m., after a long day of work, and the beginning of the week? This is just unbearable. I don't know what else to do with you and, of course, now you're going to have a puppy face as if it's my fault for us to be arguing. Why don't you just keep your mouth shut?" Bob doesn't respond, and quickly moves toward the living room.

For the next hour, Jeff tells Bob how often he says the wrong thing at the wrong time, and how he needs to relax himself with a stiff drink because it helps him control himself and fall asleep. Bob doesn't say a word; it's as if he's paralyzed, confused, and numb; he looks at his phone and reads his earlier text: "What time will you be home so I can have dinner ready for us?"

Jeff continues drinking and complaining about Bob's inappropriate text.

Here is the issue: at some point, you have learned to handle the emotional turmoil that comes with dealing with other people and upsetting life situations by using quick responses that simply feel good in the moment, distract you from your pain, and even make it go away for a couple of moments. All of these quick fixes, such as drinking, acting out sexually, or excessively focusing on your job, work so well, and feel so good, that you go back to them over and over; in a sense, you *overlearn* them.

IF YOU'RE HAPPY AND YOU KNOW IT, EAT A SNACK

Recently, when going over different ways a client handles difficulties at work with her boss, she reminded me about an old commercial from Weight Watchers. Recognize this song? "If you're happy and you know it, clap your hands . . . " In the commercial, the song was modified to:

> If you're happy and you know, eat a snack.
> If you're angry and you know it, eat a snack.
> If you're sad, and you know it, eat a snack.

When you're hurting, it does make sense that you will do anything you can to get rid of your discomfort, and escaping to a place that's more enjoyable and pleasing is always an option. Do you ever escape from a distressful feeling by using your favorite snacks, treats, or food to calm yourself? Or do you manage those crushing feelings by avoiding eating or even counting how many pieces of a food item you consume?

Distressful feelings are caused by all types of things that happen outside of you and within you; sometimes, super-feelers get troubled by how they feel when looking at their body or particular body areas or by the bodily sensations that come along with looking at different food items.

SHOPPING

> Every time Anastasia had an argument with her mom and felt frustrated by it, she quickly went to the mall to buy herself a pair of shoes or a purse. Her closet had more than twenty purses of fancy brands and thirty pairs of stilettos; together, they totaled $25,000.

When Anastasia lost her job six months ago, she went back to live with her parents because she couldn't afford the cost of living alone, and she started taking online classes to improve her career. Spending $25,000 in purses and shoes was significantly over what she could financially afford.

Anastasia had a long history of problems with her mom, feeling unseen, unheard, and compared with her sister; every time they had an argument, regardless of how it started, Anastasia felt like her body went into fire mode and she could even visibly see the signs of it when looking at herself in the mirror. "It's a combination of things I feel in the moment, like angry and frustrated," she said. Over the years, Anastasia learned to get out of that emotional hell by soothing herself with things she enjoyed the most: purses and stilettos. Even though she couldn't afford them, it was a quick fix.

Have you been in Anastasia's shoes at some point or another?

TO BE ALIVE, TO BE DEAD, OR TO CUT

Dorothy: When I turn thirty, I'll stop my pain.
Matt: I'll finish my life on Valentine's Day.
Chris: When my mom dies, then I'll commit suicide.
Stephanie: The day my kid turns eighteen, then I'll put a stop to my suffering.

These are some of the announcements made by super-feelers at some point in their lives. Going through emotional hell is exhausting for super-feelers, and their sensitivity to rejection, abandonment, and other ongoing negative feelings is so intense that all they want is a way out of it.

A client of mine, Joe, told me once: "I have been in misery since I was twelve. I'm thirty-three and I'm here, still in misery; my misery doesn't go away." Asking more about Joe's struggle, I learned that he often goes through intense feelings of loneliness and despair. He becomes so overwhelmed by these feelings and doesn't know any other way to interrupt them except by cutting his wrists, sometimes with a single cut, sometimes with multiple cuts.

Who wouldn't come up with thoughts about suicide or urges to cut when every struggle feels like a third-degree burn? It's a hard place to be when the emotional switch is on and you have been living an emotional roller coaster of intense emotions. At some point, your inner voice says, "There is no point in trying; my life is over."

Fantasy Island: Trying to Stop Your Feelings

Another way super-feelers manage their unpleasant feelings is by trying to just stop what they feel. But did you ever place your hand at the mouth of a water faucet while it's running, as if trying to keep the water from coming out? If not, I would highly recommend that you go to a sink and turn on the faucet. Let the water run, and after a couple of seconds, place your hand, palm up, on the faucet and press against the water. What happens? You just made a mess, didn't you? Every time I do this exercise, the water sprays all over. Similarly, when we're trying to suppress emotions, they gush out all over.

Here is something to keep in mind: each emotion is a multilayered experience. You don't have to take my word for it, just check with your experience right now. Bring to mind a sweet memory you had last week, hold it for a couple of moments, and notice the different aspects of the emotional experience: reactions in your body, feelings that come along, the intensity of those emotions, the thoughts that show up in your mind, and even the go-to actions you had in those moments.

What did you notice? Emotions have micro-components, including thoughts, body sensations, urges, and images, and as complex as they look, they have a beginning and an end. If you let them be, without doing anything about them, as you just did in this previous exercise, they come and they go. You don't need to be trapped in emotional misery. The challenge is that some feelings can be so distressing at times that you try to stop them. However, every time you try to suppress those uncomfortable emotions, other painful feelings appear and you're trapped in an emotional loop.

Can you tell yourself to be happy, or sad, or angry in this moment? How did it work? Quite likely, it didn't. Trying to suppress your feelings is like getting a ticket to Fantasy Island, because it is a fantasy to believe you can control, stop, or block your emotions. You don't have control of what you feel; you feel what you feel. You only have control over your actions when you're caught in the grip of self-defeating emotions.

Long-Term Solutions

Running away from your pain by drinking alcohol, having sex, overworking, soothing yourself with food, buying things you can't afford, cutting, planning the perfect time to commit suicide, or trying to stop what you feel, are all understandable responses given the amount of emotional agony you experience at times. These aren't the ideal responses, and yet, they're understandable.

Here is a key question for you: how do these quick fixes work in the long run? Do they help you be the person you want to be? What happens to your relationships?

Let's step back together and see if you can look at your private mirror by completing the following exercise.

Exercise: Inventory of Quick Fixes

Do your best to complete the following chart, looking at times in your life when you used quick fixes as a kid, teenager, young adult, and currently.

Situation	Quick Fix	Long-Term Result for You and Others Involved

As super-feeler, when you're in pain, you understandably do everything you can to get out of your emotional hell. The challenge is that all those quick fixes only work in the short term; it's a matter of time until your emotional switch gets turned on again, those unbearable emotions get activated, and you're back exactly where you were before, harassed by those feelings and doing everything you can to get rid of them.

Here is the paradox: the more you try to escape from those painful feelings or quickly take action based on them, the more you get trapped in a loop that makes your pain worse in the long term. Once you start the cycle of emotionally escaping, you get hooked on a pattern that maintains itself and takes you far away from being the best version of yourself. All emotions are acceptable, but not all behaviors are effective for you in the long run.

Here you are today, reading this book, and maybe still feeling the emptiness of not having the life you want to have. As unbelievable as it may seem, making a shift from where you are to where you want to be is possible. There are other options.

Change Is Possible

Eleven years ago, I worked with a client who attempted suicide five times in less than six months. He was in so much pain that no words could describe what he went through and how it felt to be in his shoes every time he reached a place of despair to the point of giving up. With time, showing up consistently to our meetings, and tons of effort, he learned to handle his pain using every skill I taught him. He went from being lost and giving up on life to being the father of two children, owner of a company, an incredible husband, and a solid friend for people around him. Our work wasn't easy; it was full of troubleshooting over and over about how to handle all those awful emotions, interactions with others, daily life stressors, dating issues, family pressures, and more. When I look back, I can tell you that we went back and forth multiple times about every difficulty he encountered. His life today speaks for itself, the outcome of our work together. He is no longer my client, as he can now manage his life without therapy.

Whatever degree of emotional misery you're going through, change is possible. This book will show you step by step how to tame your emotional machinery. You have new opportunities ahead of you and a life to live.

Chapter 3: New Opportunities: Acceptance and Commitment Therapy for Super-Feelers

Acceptance and Commitment Therapy (ACT) is a particular type of cognitive behavioral therapy. Developed by Hayes, Strosahl, and Wilson (1999), it has undergone more than 136 randomized clinical trials, which are considered to be the gold standard of clinical research, and it has demonstrated its applicability and efficacy in the treatment of multiple psychological struggles (Hayes 2016).

ACT invites you to do three core things: accept, choose, and take action in your life. As a super-feeler, you are invited to apply ACT principles to your life by first, *learning to notice, have, and accept* those uncomfortable emotions, thoughts, memories, sensations, and urges that come along when your emotional switch is on without trying to escape from them by using quick fixes, fantasizing about controlling them, or quickly acting based on them. Second, you learn to *choose* what truly matters to you by examining your values. And finally, you learn to *take specific behavioral steps* in your daily life toward your values while having that uncomfortable inside noise at times.

"What we practice grows" was the take-home message of a talk I attended; this saying applies to behavioral therapy at its core, and especially to ACT, because only by taking action toward becoming the person you want to be will you discover a life that is full of purpose, connection, and the potential to be the best version of yourself. ACT doesn't offer you a perfect life that is free of intense emotions or an emotional switch that turns on and off, but it certainly helps you let go of the unending and exhausting fight against painful internal experiences.

Will ACT Work for You?

I'm not a researcher or an academician. I'm a clinical psychologist by training, with expertise in empirically supported treatments, and a passionate behavioral therapist. I see clients five days a week, and I have done my best to include in this book the ACT skills that I have found help super-feelers make a shift in their life, along with the added benefits of contextual behavioral and neuro-affective sciences.

I know that the life of a super-feeler can seem like a life in hell at times because the emotions drag you from the top to the bottom, and from the bottom to the top again. I have witnessed firsthand the pain my clients go through when the emotional switch is on, and as hard and as impossible as it sounds, I have seen them make radical shifts from a super-feeler with no training to handle emotions to a super-feeler with the expertise of an emotion strategist. My clients have learned to tame their emotional machinery, handle the feelings that come and go without being consumed by them, and create incredible lives for them and the people they learned to love.

We encounter hundreds of bumps in this path of change, and we troubleshoot hundreds of times too. We never stop, and when my clients feel like giving up, as you may feel at times, I remind them about those precious moments when they were the person they wanted to be and they chose what mattered to them — even when they were hurting and their emotional switch was on. You can make a shift, too!

I'm not claiming to have the answers for every person struggling with emotion regulation difficulties, but the only way to find out whether ACT is helpful to you is by trying the skills that are offered in these chapters, choosing the ones that work you, and practicing them every day.

This book, from the first page to the last, is all about helping you be the best version of yourself, as a super-feeler. The first step is clarifying your values, so you can work toward living a life that matters to you.

Chapter 4: Clarifying Your Values: Vivir Mi Vida La La La!

Life is for living, and you can live your life by keeping yourself busy with managing your feelings, paying bills, doing things you have to do, taking action as your emotions push you to do, keeping up with your daily routine, using quick fixes when getting hurt, and so on, or you can live your life by making the best use of the limited amount of time you have on earth by doing what really matters to you. No one can make that choice for you: it's really up to you.

What Are Your Values?

Values is a word that gets thrown around a great deal these days, and it means different things to different people. Within ACT, values are the response to key questions: Are you living the life you want to live? What sort of person do you want to be? Are you the relative you want to be? Are you doing what matters to you as a friend? Are you treating yourself the way you really, deeply in your heart, want?

For the purposes of this book, and to figure out what really matters to you, here is a question: Why are you alive?

What are you here for? If you weren't so busy handling those intense emotions and the consequences of acting based on them, what would you be doing with your life? Take a moment to pause and think about this question. It's okay if you don't have all the answers.

Most of the time, we go through life on autopilot, doing the same things day after day, going through the motions, and at some point, we realize that we don't have much time left. Moving forward, you're asked to pause and make the best of your life every moment, every day, by living with intention and purpose, by living your values.

Your values are your deepest wishes and desires about the qualities you want to have in your life; they are your life's GPS. At their core, they provide the direction toward the path you need to take. Walking without knowing where you're walking and without having a firm direction in life makes you vulnerable to be the puppet of your emotional machinery and kills the time left in the bank account of your life. Consider these questions.

ARE VALUES THE WHY OR THE WHAT?

Values are the "why" of what you do, and they're different than goals. Goals are actions that are completed and checked off from a list. For instance, Rebecca, as a mother, identifies her value as "being caring" and her goals are to 1) to prepare a meal for her daughter three times a week, 2) drive her daughter to school twice a week, and 3) attend her daughter's volleyball games on the weekends. In essence, Rebecca sets her goals/actions in line with her values; her actions may change, but her values don't.

ARE VALUES FEELINGS?

A former client said, "I know I love him, because I feel it." That sentence sounds good to the ear but the challenge is that you don't have control over how you feel in a given moment; feelings come and go like waves in the ocean. We are all wired to experience a full range of emotions — that's our natural makeup — but experiencing one feeling versus another does not mean you're living your values; you're just feeling. Living your values is not about feeling good all the time; in fact, doing what matters comes with uncomfortable feelings at times. For instance, for Joe, being caring with his relatives is a core value; every month he travels for six hours to spend a weekend with his ninety-year-old grandmother, who cannot travel, barely recognizes him, and requires assistance at all times. As soon as he arrives, Joe changes her clothing, grooms her, reads her a favorite book, and shares pictures of the great-grandchildren. Even when she calls him by the wrong name, he holds her hand. Joe feels sad and frustrated, and he believes it is unfair that a woman who raised nine children is slowly dying. Yet even though performing these actions in service of his values makes him uncomfortable, he does them.

WHERE DO YOUR VALUES COME FROM?

A government, a culture, and a society each prescribe specific rules, behaviors, and even social norms for a group. Just because you belong to a group or grew up listening to specific life principles for that group doesn't mean they're your values. For example, as a Latin person, I can tell you that most Latin people grow up hearing that you should love everyone in your in-law's family. However, holding on with white knuckles to the value of "love" without discriminating, and whether or not your in-laws behave kindly and respectfully toward you, creates a one-sided relationship that is not conducive to a real connection with your in-laws. Living the values of someone or something else is not really living a values-driven life. Your personal values come directly from what matters to you and nobody else.

ARE VALUES ABOUT AVOIDING A FEELING?

A client told me once that being funny was a very important value for him; when I asked more about it, he responded that by telling a joke and being funny, he will be liked by others and create a good impression. When asked about what will happen if he's not funny, he said that he will be worried about not being liked and will even be afraid of people leaving him. As you can see, acting funny was not a value but emotional escapism for my client. He was avoiding the feeling of being disliked or abandoned by others. Values based on running away from painful emotions are like dead words, like cadaveric values.

ARE VALUES ABOUT FEELING GOOD?

If your mind says that the outcome you want in life is to feel less pain, to have less intense and distressful emotions like anxiety or sadness, or to feel happiness and peace at all times, I totally get it; it's understandable because it's hard to be a super-feeler. Now, let me break the news: those are also dead goals because, as much you wish it were true, you don't have control over what you feel; you feel what you feel. But you do have control over how you act and how you really want to live your life.

Now that we have gone over a few considerations about values, what about figuring out yours? The exercise below is not fancy, but it's a beginning to find your personal GPS. Make the best of it!

Exercise: Choosing Your Values

Let's step back in time to five different moments in your life when you were being yourself and not what your emotional machinery was pushing you to be. Grab a piece of paper and write about five different moments when you were being just YOU. Think about times when you felt comfortable in your own skin, had a sense of vitality, and felt alive, when you were doing what speaks deeply to you, and in that moment, life was just perfect. Write down the situation, the person you were with, and what you were doing. Imagine that someone was videotaping you in those moments: What would they see in the camera?

After recalling and writing about these five different memories, see if there are any qualities that stand out to you across all of them. Those are your values. Write them down, keeping in mind that your values are verbs. You don't need to have a shopping list of your values, just a refined list of what you strive to be and stand for in your personal life.

For instance, after completing this exercise, Anne came up with the following values: being caring, down-to-earth, and authentic.

Values, and how to live your life, have been the source of inspiration for writers, poets, artists, and musicians like Marc Anthony and Coldplay; our values keep us going when we're hurting, and we hurt because our values are not fulfilled at times in our life.

A life based on your values is about . . .

Doing the Doing

Living your values is a verb, not a string of nice words on a piece of paper. Taking steps toward what matters to you gives you a new way of being in the world; it is not pain free, but it means you get to choose how you want to live your life instead of your emotions choosing for you and dragging you around in the process. The more steps you take toward becoming the person you want to be, the better it gets, and as they say, "What you practice grows."

DESPACITO: STEP BY STEP

The word *despacito* in Spanish means "slowly." You may wonder what it has to do with this chapter. Living your values is all about taking step-by-step actions toward your values, even if that's *despacito*. Living your values is not about how fast you walk in life, or how perfectly you do it; it's about choosing over and over how to live.

You cannot live your values by taking actions in random directions. As one of my clients said, "You cannot explore San Francisco driving in the streets of Seattle." Living a values-based life is like taking steps toward your destination: your values. The rest is just noise.

How do you do it? By answering the three "*w* questions": what, when, and with whom. For instance, Anne decided to live her value of being a caring daughter when her mom was struggling with Alzheimer's disease by spending every Saturday with her, even when her mother didn't recognize her, or thought she was her cousin, or didn't talk at all. Anne drove two hours every Saturday to spend the day with her mom, even when she had thoughts like "She doesn't even know who I am," "Does she know what I'm doing?" "How did this happen to her?" and "It's not fair." In the end, Anne wouldn't trade those Saturdays for anything; thinking about caring for her mom during her last days gives her so much joy.

No matter how far or close you are from where you want to be, you can choose your next steps with intention and move toward what really matters. This doesn't mean it is always going to be easy to take values-based actions; in fact, some days you may feel like your emotions are pulling you in different directions. You may find yourself quite far from who you really want to be, but I promise that the more you move toward what matters, the better your life will be. Try it!

Living Your Values

Let me briefly share a mini story with you. After dealing with a history of chronic depression, alcohol problems, and cutting behaviors as a teen, Darcy found herself in a high-conflict marriage. Every time Darcy and her husband fought, she was told that it was her fault; she learned to respond to her husband's anger with anger, countering his character attacks with another attack, and responding to his disconnection with more disconnection.

When discussing with Darcy what really hurt in those arguments it was clear that she was in pain because she valued "kindness" as a very important personal quality; she didn't like herself going into angry mode, criticizing, fighting back, and screaming at her husband. In an attempt to live her values, and not knowing how her husband would respond, Darcy made a goal of showing kindness toward herself by checking whether it was worth it to continue the argument or not. Every time they had a fight, Darcy told her husband, "I see you're upset, and I'm upset too. I need to pause because we're just hurting each other." Sometimes, Darcy's husband chose to pause along with her; sometimes, he went on screaming; and other times, he left the house very angry.

Darcy realized that acting with kindness toward herself was not about how her husband responded to her, but rather how she wanted to be, especially when she was upset with him and they were arguing. She didn't want to become an angry woman. Each time Darcy asked to pause in the middle of the fight, she noticed this unique feeing of joy about choosing to be the person she wanted to be: a kind person. It wasn't easy, and certainly not pain free, and yet it was priceless to her.

You can only live your values with your feet, with your behavior, with what you do. As a super-feeler, your emotions pull you in all directions. But I promise you that stepping back, checking your values, and choosing your behavior will make a difference.

There is no better personal GPS in your life than your values.

SECTION ❙❙

Me and My Emotions

Chapter 5: What Are Emotions?

Now that you've learned more about how you became a super-feeler, identified some of the quick fixes you may have relied on at times, and discovered the consequences of them in your life, let's dive more deeply into the whole business of emotions and how they work. After all, if you're a super-feeler, it's important to understand how that engine is driving you.

Emotional Machinery

Emotions are systems with multiple parts, like a large and rich machinery where physiology, neurology, and psychology act together, all at once, and all the time; when one element of this emotional machinery gets activated, all parts of it start a fascinating operation. We carry our emotional machinery with us wherever we go: it's always there.

When the switch of the emotional machinery is turned on, different systems are orchestrated within our body: the sympathetic, parasympathetic, endocrine, and neurological systems all coordinate what goes on in our body. It also coordinates micro-psychological processes that show up all at once: your attention, thoughts, memories, images, and impulses. It's the interaction of all these systems that puts your behavior in motion: you act.

Emotions don't come out of the blue. They get started by an encounter — the spike of joy you feel when looking at a three-day holiday weekend coming up on the calendar, the excitement you have when staring at your favorite dish on a menu, the sadness you feel when your basketball team loses, or the anger you experience when the people you love get hurt. Emotions can also get started from internal activities, such as remembering your first kiss, fantasizing about the next trip you're going to take, or worrying that no one is going to read your book.

Every feeling we experience has a life of its own, and like mini systems, they are formed by granular components. For instance, in this moment of writing, when I look within, I feel an intense sense of joy, along with my heart beating fast and a warm temperature on my cheeks (physical sensations); an image of my old apartment (memory); random questions such as "Is this enough? Is it too short?" (thoughts); and a strong urge to type as fast as I can on the laptop before the ideas run away from my mind (impulse).

Right now, as you're reading this book, wherever you are, pause and notice the micro-components of your emotional machinery. Can you notice what types of thoughts, memories, or images your mind is coming up with? Is your body making any noise, or is there a predominant feeing right now? Do you have an urge to do something in this moment?

Here is another important piece of information about emotions: they usually last only seconds, believe it or not. Feelings have a fleeting presence in general, and they dissipate until the next one comes. It's only when we dwell, ruminate, or ponder about the why of an emotion or an event that their duration is extended. For instance, Charlie spilled wine on his friend's sweater by accident. Even though his friend understood that it was an accident and told him not to worry about it,

Charlie felt embarrassed and spent hours wondering why he spilled the wine, why he didn't pay more attention, what if his friend didn't like him any longer, and so on.

Having an uncomfortable emotion doesn't mean necessarily acting based on it. When the emotional switch is on, uncomfortable emotions feel like a third-degree burn and demand immediate attention. Taking action based on the intense feelings of the moment, without checking in on whether the situation calls for action and what's really important in the long run is what gets us into trouble.

Here is a scenario about Troy, a super-feeler, and how his emotional machinery drives his reactions:

> *Troy (angry tone of voice): "Why didn't you call me? I called you six times but got no response. You don't know how worried I was."*
>
> *Pamela: "I'm sorry. I forgot to turn my cell phone on after yoga class. I totally forgot to turn it on, and then I went to run errands."*
>
> *Troy (angry tone of voice): "You know how worried I get about you; I was concerned something bad happened to you. I didn't know what was going on. You were just gone, and here I was trying to make sure you were safe."*
>
> *Pamela: "I totally get that you got worried and didn't have a way to get ahold of me. I'm sorry; sometimes I just forget things. Can I just ask for a kiss of peace, so we can move on, please?"*
>
> *Troy (screaming): "There is no way I'm going to kiss you right now! I'm canceling our dinner plans and telling your family we're not going to hang out with them tonight!"*

Did you notice how Troy's emotions escalated quickly and in a way that had longer-term consequences? Where did those strong emotions come from? Let's do a brief exercise so you can notice the history of your emotional landscape.

Exercise: History of Your Emotions

Set aside 10 minutes for this exercise. Find a quiet place, sit as comfortably as possible, and read the directions over, so you know what's expected before beginning. You can also record yourself reading the instructions in a soft voice and at a slow pace.

In the next couple of moments, bring your awareness to your breathing, noticing every time you breathe in and breathe out. Notice the air coming into your nostrils, moving into your diaphragm, and slowly leaving your body with every exhalation. Give yourself a couple of moments and then choose an emotion to focus on for this exercise; it can be sadness, loneliness, envy, or any feeling. Pick a feeling that is not too problematic for you, so you can still work on it for this exercise.

After choosing a feeling, see if you can go back in time to a moment in your childhood when you experienced this particular emotion. There is no need to get distracted by trying to choose the perfect situation; simply do your best to choose a memory. Give yourself some time to bring this memory into your mind as vividly as possible, recalling the specifics of it, and see if you can stay with this image for a couple of moments. Take your time and do your best to allow yourself to pay attention to this image. Scan your body from head to toe and pay attention to some common areas, such as your tummy, chest, shoulders, throat, or jaw.

Next, let this memory go, and direct your attention back to your breathing; intentionally slow it down so you center yourself by breathing in and breathing out for 10 seconds.

Go back to a particular moment as a teenager in which you experienced the emotion you're working on; as you did with the first memory, don't get distracted by trying to choose the perfect situation. Again, notice the specifics of the situation, how it felt in that moment, and any thoughts, urges, and physical sensations related to it. If you can, hold that memory in mind for a little bit longer than before. Scan your body from head to toe and pay attention to some common areas, such as your tummy, chest, shoulders, throat, or jaw.

After a couple of moments, gently let this image fade from your mind, and bring your awareness to your breathing: focus on every time you breathe in and breathe out.

Finally, go to a time in your young adult life. See if you can recall another memory in which this feeling was present. When bringing that image into your mind, as you did with the other images, scan your body from head to toe and pay attention to some common areas, such as your tummy, chest, shoulders, throat, or jaw.

After taking a couple of slow and deep breaths, slowly bring yourself back and notice your surroundings.

What did you notice when completing this exercise? How did it feel to notice a particular emotion throughout different times in your life? Did you handle it similarly or differently? Here is another key question: Did you notice the difference between *the feeling* and yourself as *the person having the feeling*?

By simply watching your emotions, without trying to change or suppress them, you will learn to have your feelings without becoming them. Your emotions come and go, rise and fall, hundreds of times each day; they're dynamic and have tons of variations in intensity, degree, and pace.

Your feelings are your feelings, and you can learn to have them, hold them, contain them, and carry them without becoming the feeler that takes action on every emotion that shows up. Your feelings are your feelings; they're not you.

The Bad Rap About Negative Emotions

Most of the emotions you focus on are probably the uncomfortable and overwhelming ones, which is why you try so hard to suppress or change them. But our beliefs or misconceptions about feelings make them even more unbearable. Let's go over some common beliefs about uncomfortable feelings.

BELIEF: "PAINFUL EMOTIONS LAST FOREVER."

Emotions don't last forever, and that applies to the unpleasant, aggravating, and upsetting emotions as well. When left alone, emotions pass in a matter of minutes. It's hard to believe, and yet the research from affective science has been very consistent about it. Emotions have a time-limited life, but when you spend hours chewing on them you end up getting trapped by all types of mind noise that amplifies your feelings and makes them last longer.

BELIEF: "INTENSE FEELINGS ARE OTHER PEOPLE'S FAULT."

"If she didn't text me so late, I wouldn't be so mad," you might think. Here is the deal: others' behaviors could certainly be the catalyst for your intense emotions; however, when others encounter a similar situation, they're not necessarily carried away by their emotion as you are. There is something unique about this situation to you; you are the only one having the emotional experience, regardless of what started it.

BELIEF: "EXPRESSING MY INTENSE FEELINGS IS ALWAYS HEALTHY."

Identifying what an emotion is trying to communicate to you, as you'll learn in this book, is very different than talking about it over and over to different people, journaling more than twenty pages about it, or mulling about it repeatedly. Those are all responses that actually amplify the intensity and duration of the feelings, and they make them last longer and exercise the rumination muscle. For instance, research on anger demonstrates that venting anger will simply make you more upset. Blowing off steam is simply not beneficial for your mind or body, and it will not help your relationships (Tavris 1989).

BELIEF: "DISTRESSING EMOTIONS ALWAYS POINT ME TOWARD WHAT I NEED TO DO."

While it is certainly true that intense emotions communicate to you and others what's important to you, acting quickly based on them — without pausing, stepping back, and evaluating a situation for what matters — can actually be hurtful to you and the people you love. Experiencing intense feelings is one thing, but behaving without first distinguishing whether your actions will be effective or not is a different story.

BELIEF: "ALL UNCOMFORTABLE EMOTIONS ARE BAD FOR ME."

Distressing emotions are hard to sit with and feel very painful at times, like a third-degree burn. Here is a caveat: having these uncomfortable emotions doesn't mean that it's bad — uncomfortable, yes, but not always terrible. At times, those painful feelings may be actually conveying important messages about what matters to you in regard to a particular situation.

Now that we've covered the bad rap about troubling emotions, see if you can identify the beliefs that resonate with you and be aware of them when troublesome situations come up.

Emotional Noise

We all experience emotions, all types of them, and with a broad range of intensity, variability, and speed; it's as if our emotional machinery makes emotional noise, all the time.

Let's start with the basics of noticing your feelings, so you can begin to distinguish the various components of this emotional noise: emotional reactions, physical sensations, thoughts, images, memories, and urges to take action.

Exercise: Noticing Your Emotional Noise

This exercise has two parts, and each takes about 5 minutes to complete.

Part 1.
Choose one of your favorite songs, prepare to play it, grab a piece of paper, and after finding a comfortable position, set a timer to

listen to this song for 2 minutes. When the timer goes off, grab your journal, and answer the following questions:

- ❑ What were some of the reactions you noticed in your body?
- ❑ Did you notice any particular sensation? Was this sensation static or was it moving?
- ❑ What emotion or emotions came up? Can you name them?
- ❑ Did any thoughts, images, or memories accompany these sensations and emotions?
- ❑ What did you feel like doing when listening to this song?
- ❑ Did you feel any attempts to change, suppress, or escape your emotions?

Sometimes my clients struggle with naming the emotion, so if necessary, take a look at any list of emotions on the internet.

Part 2.
Set the timer for 2 minutes, close your eyes, and bring to mind a mildly difficult situation you encountered last week; it can be a situation that happened at work or school, with friends or relatives. Do your best to bring that situation to mind as vividly as possible. Pay attention to it, notice the details of it, the sounds of it, and the specifics of that particular challenging moment. Then, answer the same questions that you did for the first part of the exercise.

For instance, Shelly recalled a phone conversation she had with her mother, Amanda, and how disappointed she felt after learning that Amanda wasn't going to visit her. Shelly noticed how her chest quickly contracted and she had a strong impulse to tell her mom how selfish and inconsiderate she was for not coming

to visit her, despite her multiple requests over the years. Shelly noticed how strong and overwhelming these impulses were while talking on the phone and even afterward.

Did you notice that an emotional experience is not a static surface? It actually has granular components: bodily sensations, urges to do something, and thoughts, and they all come at once. Keep in mind that when I say "thoughts," I'm referring to images and memories as well, not just words or a stream of words. Every emotion we experience is actually a microsystem. As a super-feeler, you experience hundreds of those emotional microsystems throughout the day, one feeling after another, and you experience them at a maximum level and at a fast pace.

Here is the second observation that I would like to bring to your attention with this exercise: when you notice your emotions you are actually describing the feeling, sensations, thoughts, urges, and images that go along with them. Saying things like "I notice an awful memory" is not noticing, but saying, "I notice the memory of my car breaking down" is noticing.

Noticing What Is What

Read the quotations below describing two different reactions to hearing about Hurricane Irma in Florida:

- "I was shocked, sad, and worried about everyone in Florida, and then I had the urgency to do something about it."
- "I cannot recall exactly what happened; all I know is that I felt a collection of things and the next thing I knew I was feeling down."

What did you notice? The first person described specific emotional reactions, and the second one made a vague statement about her experience. Why does it matter? A study conducted by Kashdan et al. (2015) at George Mason University in Fairfax, Virginia, with individuals struggling with social anxiety, found that people who experience distressful feelings and cannot distinguish them for what they are have a higher likelihood of engaging in other types of unhelpful regulatory responses, such as binge drinking or aggression.

How does this finding apply to the world of super-feelers? Super-feelers feel too intensely, too quickly. This means that you become overwhelmed by not knowing how to solve a problem because everything feels cumbersome; however, learning to pause and identify what set off the emotional machinery makes a big difference in your response. When everything feels complicated, try to notice the starting point. Ask yourself, what was the first emotion that started my emotional machinery?

Core Skill: Noticing and Naming Your Emotions

Naming your emotions as a skill sounds like a simplistic and almost insignificant task, but you will be shocked to read the evidence behind it and how helpful it is when the emotional switch is on.

Craske et al. (2014) conducted a study looking at the impact of labeling emotions with people struggling with a fear of spiders. All participants received a general instruction: to get as close as possible to touching a spider, but after being divided into four groups, they received different instructions about how to handle their emotions based on the group they were assigned to:

■ The first group was instructed to label their feelings about the spider as they appeared (e.g., I'm anxious, scared, etc.).

- The second group was asked to think differently about the spider so it wouldn't feel as threatening (e.g., spiders can't hurt me, this spider is small, etc.).
- The third group was asked to distract themselves from their emotions about the spider.
- The fourth group didn't receive any instruction.

The participants' physiological reactivity was measured immediately and a week after the experiment. Which group do you think got closer to the spider and which group had less physiological reactivity? To everyone's surprise, the first group that labeled their emotions as they came up showed fewer physiological signs of anxiety and got closer to the spider.

How is this possible? Naming your emotional state decreases the activity in the amygdala, the organ in your brain that is in charge of your emotional reactions. The skill of naming your emotions will help you turn down your overactive amygdala. Noticing your emotions for what they are, as they come, and naming them are core skills to navigate the emotional machinery when it's activated, especially when you're hurting. But you may wonder, if emotions are so painful, why do we have them in the first place? That is the subject of the next chapter.

Chapter 6: What Is the Function of Emotions?

I was having dinner with a colleague of mine, and while discussing a workshop he was going to attend, he looked into my eyes and with conviction said, "We're emotional beings." It was something that we both knew, but it was the prompt I needed to write about one of the most fascinating topics of the complexity of human beings: our emotional landscape.

Antonio Damasio was the first neurologist to question the supremacy of thinking, acknowledge the function of emotionality, and elaborate on how emotions can support reasoning. Damasio's work with a client named Elliot was the foundation of his theory (1994).

Elliot was a successful businessman, model father, and dedicated husband who, after being diagnosed with a brain tumor, had surgery to remove it. He had an apparently successful recovery, but he couldn't perform the daily functions in life. Elliot's IQ stayed intact after the surgery, he was verbally eloquent, had appropriate memory skills, could perform math operations and sophisticated financial calculations, and yet routine tasks like choosing a pen to write with, a radio station to listen to, or a snack to eat were paralyzing for him. Damasio couldn't initially figure out why a cognitively smart man couldn't make basic decisions. Elliot ended up going through two divorces, developing money problems, losing his job, and going back to live with his parents. How was that possible?

After hundreds of hours interviewing Elliot, Damasio identified a key factor: Elliot was emotionally numb. He was always controlled and emotionally flat; he never displayed frustration, happiness, joy, or any other emotion during conversation. Damasio discovered a fundamental function of our emotions: we need them to make daily life decisions, because thinking is not enough. For example, when you're looking at a menu in a restaurant, every item sends a signal to your amygdala about what you want to eat or not, what you crave or not, and based on that emotional input and other variables, such as your thoughts about your diet and weight, you make a decision. Elliot lost the capacity to have an emotional reaction and couldn't choose what to order even though he could read the menu, understand the different dishes, and even list all possible combinations of food items. Elliot felt nothing.

Damasio's work was the beginning of a revolution in neuroscience and the acknowledgment of the role of emotions in our daily life. We're emotional beings.

Generally speaking, emotions serve important purposes for our survival as a species, as a group, and as individuals. Emotions, including the uncomfortable, annoying, and distressful ones, help us 1) communicate with others, 2) figure out what's going on with us, 3) survive dangerous situations, 4) motivate us to take action toward what's important to us, and 5) connect with others. If you do a short inventory of different periods in your life, you will likely find more than one event that shows how your emotions fulfilled each one of these functions.

Core Skill: Noticing the Function of Your Emotions

Let's look more closely at how emotions affect specific moments, situations, or contexts in your life. Noticing what starts your emotional machinery, the emotion that comes with it, and its effect is a core skill.

As you recall from earlier sections, your feelings get started by something either outside or inside you, and then you do something in a given moment. Let's take a look at this in detail.

Situation (Internal or External)	Emotional Machinery
Having a fight with boyfriend about an electricity bill	**Feelings:** Disappointed **Thoughts:** How is it possible he played so many video games? What's wrong with him? **Urges:** To talk to boyfriend
Memory of deceased grand-mother	**Feelings:** Grief **Thoughts:** I miss her so much; I wish she were here with me right now. **Urges:** To call sister to talk about grandma

Notice that a situation can be something that happens outside of you or inside of you. Now, if we break it down, when your emotional system gets activated, it becomes the antecedent, or trigger, for you to do something, to take action; this is your behavior.

Situation	Emotional Machinery	Behavior
Having a fight with boyfriend about an electricity bill	**Feelings:** Disappointed **Thoughts:** How is it possible he played so many video games? What's wrong with him? **Urges:** To tell boyfriend this is wrong	Screamed at him: What's wrong with you? Don't you see how much I'm working to pay our bills?

Your behavior has a consequence for you right away, in the moment.

Situation	Emotional Machinery	Behavior	Consequences
Having a fight with boyfriend about an electricity bill	**Feelings:** Disappointed **Thoughts:** How is it possible he played so many video games? What's wrong with him? **Urges:** To tell boyfriend this is wrong	**Screamed at him:** What's wrong with you? Don't you see how much I'm working to pay our bills?	Feeling good

Feelings come and go, and because you're dealing with high emotional sensitivity, these emotional microsystems you go through act as dictators of your behavior. Then you're left with the consequences, some of which are helpful to you, others not so much. Let's break them down into short- and long-term consequences:

Situation	Emotional Microsystem	Behavior	Consequences
Having a fight with boyfriend about an electricity bill	**Feelings:** Disappointed **Thoughts:** How is it possible he played so many video games? What's wrong with him? **Urges:** To tell boyfriend this is wrong	**Screamed at him:** What's wrong with you? Don't you see how much I'm working to pay your bills?	**Short-term consequence:** Feeling good **Long-term consequence:** Feeling bad for talking to boyfriend like that

Your emotions, as microsystems, are the triggers for your actions, and if you pay attention to their consequences, you will be able to choose an effective behavior. In short, you will chart your emotional strategy course, the subject of the next chapter.

Chapter 7: Charting an Emotional Strategy Course

When something doesn't work in your household, what do you do? You call the specialist, right? After attempting for hours to hang curtain rods in my new apartment, having the drill, the anchor, and the nail ready to go, I gave up when I noticed the three different holes in the wall and the curtain rods were still sitting on the floor. Then, I called the specialist. He came, and in less than ten minutes he had the curtain rod in place and the nice white curtains hanging in the living room. The bill was for $50. When I asked for the breakdown of it, he told me that I could have done it myself, but I was using the wrong end for the drill. The handyman's big fee wasn't for hanging the curtain rods only but because he *knew* what end was needed for the drill given the type of wall. He was the specialist.

Specialists have an expertise in a particular domain and have a strategy about how to handle different situations: they step back from a situation, study it, see what's needed, when it's needed, and how to make it happen.

In this book, you're learning about emotion strategy. Instead of letting distressful emotions stomp on you, doing what they tell you to do, and becoming a puppet of the emotional machinery, you're reading and learning specific core competences to choose how to live your life.

You have already learned different elements of your emotional machinery: challenges with using quick fixes, noticing and naming your feelings, beliefs about negative emotions, the fantasy of stopping your feelings, and lastly, the impact of your emotions on your behavior.

Here are some other core skills for you to develop and practice as you move forward.

Core Skill: Stepping Back and Pausing

Stepping back as a skill means exactly that: stepping back from a situation in your mind as if you're stepping back from it physically. I'm not asking you to check out or dissociate but to see whether, when the emotion switch is on, you can notice, describe, and name your feelings, and then step back and pause. Then you can check your values and choose how you want to behave.

For instance, when I was discussing this behavior with Shelly, a super-feeler, she stared at me and said in a somehow surprised, angry tone of voice, "Are you serious? Should I just simply let it go and bottle up my true emotions? Are you asking me to be fake with myself?"

Here is my response: choosing how to respond to both light and intense emotions doesn't make you a fake person but a wise one. Acting quickly based on the emotion, without measuring the impact of your behavior, is a recipe for disaster — for yourself, the people you love, and your relationships. If you don't care about your relationships, then that's the path to take: every time there is an emotion demanding you take action, you simply go along, without checking whether it's helpful to you or not. However, it's quite likely this will add another layer to your struggles. Simply look back at the outcomes of the times you acted based on your emotions, in an automatic mode, and decide for yourself whether this makes sense.

Learning about emotion strategy is not about developing insight, receiving magical revelations, or using touchy-feely stuff; it's about stepping back, pausing, and choosing your behavioral responses.

Core Skill: Checking and Choosing

Steve Hayes, PhD, one of the cofounders of ACT, has this sentence at the bottom of his e-mail signature: "Love is not just a thing; it's the only thing."

Here is my adaptation of it for the purposes of our work: checking your values, checking your action-urges, and choosing your behaviors are not just things; they are the only things!

No matter where we are or the time of day, we're constantly bombarded by all types of messages through the media, advertisers, friends, or significant others about how we should be: what status to pursue in life, the type of car to buy, where to travel for vacation, or what should make us happy or not. Those are not our choices.

Choosing our values is choosing what we care about, and choosing what we care about is choosing to have all types of feelings, pleasant and unpleasant ones, sweet and sour ones, comfortable and uncomfortable ones, all of them together. When Nelson Mandela chose to make his life about advocating against racial discrimination in South Africa, he was faced with a sentence of twenty-seven years in prison and all that comes with losing your freedom in society; and yet, when asked about whether he would have done something different, he stated he would do the same things over and over. Mandela was living his values, step by step and action by action.

In chapter 4 you identified your personal values. Learning to live a life that matters is not easy. It requires skills, practice, and patience. Wherever you are in life right now, whatever you have gone through, and no matter how much your emotional machinery troubles you, change is possible. But how do you do it? What does it look like in your life to practice checking and choosing? First, you ask yourself specific questions about a problematic situation:

1. Check your values:

What's my value in this situation?

2. Check the workability of your action-urges:

Is my behavior in the short term consistent with my values?
Is my behavior in the long term consistent with my values?

"Workability" is the yardstick by which you measure your behavioral choices. Choosing your behaviors can be a move away or a move toward your values depending on the situation.

For example, when choosing to avoid writing because my mind is hooked in thoughts like "you don't know what you're doing, your writing is not good enough, no one is going to read your book," I am moving away from my personal value of contributing. However, if I choose not to write because I need to spend quality time with my partner before he travels, and that's consistent with my value of connecting with the people I love, then that's a move toward my values.

If you keep getting stuck in the same situations over and over as if you're in a loop, and you keep getting the same results, then something is not working.

It's possible you are listening too much to your gut feelings. Let's check!

Chapter 8: Watch Out for Those Gut Feelings!

In 2003, *Harvard Business Review* magazine conducted a survey of executives from a private firm. The findings revealed that 45 percent of the executives relied on gut feelings more than on objective data when making decisions about their businesses. It seems reasonable, right? Maybe not.

Gut Feelings Are Overrated

The popular idea about trusting our hunches may have romanticized certain situations in everyone's life. It's quite likely that for every example of a great gut decision there's an equal example of a terrible one; we could spend hours discussing it, but that's a different book.

Here is what affective science says about gut feelings: a recent study conducted by Dane et al. (2012) indicated that despite conventional knowledge about the power of hunches, there is no relationship between individuals trusting their gut feelings and the accuracy of them when making a decision; gut feelings are extremely helpful only when expertise goes along with them. For instance, a firefighter, after participating in more than fifty rescue operations, has the expertise to trust his gut feelings, whereas a firefighter who is participating in an operation for the first time may have gut feelings pulling him in all directions and opening the possibility of making the wrong decision.

Why is this important? Because as a super-feeler, you wake up feeling something and go to bed feeling something else; it's constant emotional noise because your overactive amygdala continuously shouts at you with all types of feelings, thoughts, memories, sensations, at all types of intensities, and with a variety of go-to actions. You may distinguish particular bodily sensations, like butterflies in your stomach or a sense of hollowness in your chest. You may also identify some of them as your gut feelings or hunches, even if you cannot name them right away.

You then make sense of them by giving them meaning with your thoughts, and then you quickly act based on them without checking whether your behavior helps you move toward or against your values.

Feeling a particular emotion, or having butterflies in your stomach or a racing heart, is not a warning sign that something is going to happen or that you have to take action right away. As a super-feeler, you're more sensitive to all types of emotions; without paying attention to them, they keep you on edge, in alert mode, and are a hazard for veering off the emotional course you charted for yourself.

I'm not saying you shouldn't listen to your body; in fact, in this book you're learning that bodily sensations are granular elements of your emotions. What I am saying is that it's important for you to pause and check that so-called gut feeling before jumping to conclusions or immediately reacting to it. For instance, when your stomach makes noise, it doesn't always mean that you're hungry or in pain; sometimes it's just stomach noise.

So what do you do about it? When having a gut reaction, take a moment to pause and distinguish emotions that are true indicators of actions you need to take from the emotional noise that is coming and going constantly.

Here is a key difference: a so-called gut feeling that is an emotion indicator of an important action you need to take is more like soft music in the background, without demanding you do something right away; a gut feeling that is emotional noise is like music in a heavy metal concert: it is loud, punches you, and usually insists you do something about it immediately.

Exercise: Distinguishing Gut Reactions

Read the example below of Monica's reaction to waiting for her boyfriend Rich, and then see if you can complete this exercise for yourself:

Situation	Gut Reaction
Waiting for 30 minutes for boyfriend to return home	**Familiar sensation/emotion:** Hollow pain in my chest **Thoughts:** He's cheating on me, he's going to leave me **Behavior:** Calling him every 5 minutes, asking where he is
	Familiar sensation/ emotion: **Thoughts:** **Behavior:**

In general, when your emotion switch is on and you're in a state of hyperarousal — your heart is beating fast, your breathing is shallow, your muscles are tightening, and you have a strong itch to do something right away — it's quite likely that your emotions are not a good source for making decisions or taking action, even if those feelings are familiar to you.

Only when you're in direct and immediate danger, like someone is attacking you, you are approaching the edge of a cliff, or you are in the middle of crossing the street and a car is speeding toward you, is listening to your body an adaptive response. There is a difference between real urgency and the urgency that our emotions make us perceive.

As a super-feeler, you need to continue to pay attention to all the feelings that come along with the emotional machinery, including the "gut feelings," before getting trapped by them. One of those biggest traps is following the chain of feelings you have *about* your feelings, as you will see in the next chapter.

Chapter 9: Emotions About Emotions

> Olivia, a twenty-four-year-old college student and a super-feeler, fell in love with her boyfriend Michael. During lunchtime, Olivia notices that Laura, a classmate, has been approaching him in a way that she perceives as flirtatious: laughing, staring at him, sitting next to him, and asking for his opinion about different topics, some school related and some not. Olivia has thought about discussing her discomfort with Michael, but because of her fears about coming across as a jealous person, she has kept this reaction to herself.
>
> A day after a test, she sees Laura approach Michael and start joking with him about how athletic he is; Laura quickly places her hand on Michael's stomach. Olivia feels afraid about losing Michael, and she quickly slaps Laura across the face. She then feels embarrassed about her behavior and runs to the bathroom to hide. In the bathroom, she starts crying loudly, and in her attempt to hide her emotions, she pretends to be talking on the phone. A girl in the bathroom tells her to stop being fake. Olivia, now even more embarrassed, quickly texts her sister to come pick her up, that it is an emergency. During the drive home, she doesn't

say a word to her sister and as soon as she gets home, she runs to her bedroom. Olivia is disappointed in herself and embarrassed for bothering her sister, and she cries for hours.

Did you notice how Olivia went through a chain of emotions: scared, jealous, fearful, disappointed, and then embarrassed? Let's apply what you learned in chapter 6 by looking at this particular situation: Olivia's emotional switch went on as soon as Laura started flirting with Michael (situation). She then felt afraid of losing Michael (first emotion), quickly acted on that emotion (behavior), and that in turn led to another distressful behavior and then to another uncomfortable feeling; it was a chain of emotions, thoughts, and behaviors, one after another.

Your emotions are the fuel for your behavior: you feel them at the core and get trapped by every thought that comes along with them and then take action, but then that action becomes the trigger for another emotion that comes along with other thoughts, images, memories, and sensations, and you take action again and the chain keeps going. Sometimes this chain of feelings and behaviors can be short, and other times it can be very long. Regardless, these chains are another potential hazard for deviating from your emotional strategy course.

Exercise: Recognizing Your Emotional Chains

See if you can step back and look at three different situations in which you went through emotion after emotion by completing the following chart:

Triggering Situation	First Emotion	Behavior	Second Emotion	Behavior	Third Emotion	Behavior

For super-feelers, it's very helpful to notice how overwhelming feelings drive behaviors that can easily become the catalyst for an endless chain of painful emotions, thoughts, memories, sensations, and problematic behaviors. It's already hard to feel what you feel; it's even harder to get trapped by emotion about the emotion.

Every day, start by paying attention to the triggering situation and the first emotional reaction you have (your primary emotion). From there, pause, check your values, and check if your urges to take action take you closer or further away from your personal values. Then choose your behavior, before you end up in cranky town.

Chapter 10: Cranky Town

A former client shared with me, "When I was a kid, I learned that if I show an angry face and scream louder than my father, he will stop yelling at me or asking me to do things for him; so that's what I did."

Naturally, as a kid, my client knew only to act based on his impulses in the heat of the moment, like responding to anger with anger, until whatever was upsetting him stopped. The challenge was that my client quickly applied this learning to all situations when someone did or said something upsetting. He basically overlearned a behavior, and without distinguishing the situation or the relationship, he responded the same way with his friends, dates, coworkers, and relatives. Over the years, he ended up with a long list of failed relationships, broken friendships, and months or years of disconnection from his siblings.

Like dinosaurs, lost cities and old artifacts, anger has long been a subject of fascination. Psychologists are driven to study it because of how often it shows up and how quickly it affects many people on a daily basis. Could you imagine how many people are angry at this very moment while you are reading this book?

Anger is a valid, authentic, genuine emotion and a sticky one at the same time; left to its own devices and without monitoring, it could color all interactions you have with yourself and others. If you get sidetracked by anger, you won't be staying on your emotional strategy course.

Let's dig into it.

Exercise: Studying Your Anger Hazards

Let's identify the *anger hazards* that show up in your daily life. To start, make a list of anger-provoking situations that trigger you over and over. Now, choose a particular anger hazard to work on for this exercise.

Because this is the first time you're completing this exercise, it's best if you choose a situation that is mildly upsetting. When you're ready, do your best to recall it and hold the image of this angry memory in your mind for a couple of minutes, as if you're really discovering and exploring it for the first time. Give yourself some time to notice all the aspects of that angry situation in your mind. Then, answer the following questions:

1. What button was pushed in me? Why does it make me so upset?
2. What are those angry thoughts showing up? Are there any judgment thoughts about me or others involved? Are there any expectations or rules that were broken? Are there any future-oriented thoughts?
3. Do I notice any sensation or body reaction in that moment? Do I feel any type of discomfort?
4. What did I end up doing because of the anger?
5. Key question: Was my behavior consistent with my personal values?

See if you can repeat this exercise with other anger-provoking situations. The main purpose is to identify your hot buttons, the ones that are unique to you and no one else. Is there a theme across those buttons? Do they have similarities, or are the hot buttons all different?

Beliefs About Anger

Anger, as sticky and strong as it is, can also be misleading because of all the fabrications that have been accumulating about it over the years in pop psychology and not very scientific communities. Let's take a look at the most common beliefs about it that may be creating anger hazards for you.

BELIEF: "IF SHE HADN'T SAID THAT, I WOULDN'T BE UPSET; MY ANGER IS OTHERS' FAULT."

While other people's behaviors clearly make you angry, you're the one who goes through those angry thoughts, feelings, sensations, and memories. You're the owner of your response and how to handle your angry feelings; no one can do that for you. Others hear the same words, see the same situation, and yet they are not carried away by anger. Whatever others say, it's your hot button, not theirs.

BELIEF: "IF I GET ANGRY, I GET WHAT I WANT; ANGER IS THE ONLY WAY TO MANAGE OTHER PEOPLE'S BEHAVIOR."

While feeling angry is a very authentic feeling, acting based on it might quickly give you what you want but it could also damage your relationships with the people you care about. Screaming, giving ultimatums, or disconnecting from a person doesn't help with solving a conflict; in fact, it simply makes the situation worse. There are other ways to ask for what you want, without hurting others and hurting yourself.

BELIEF: "EXPRESSING ANGER IS ALWAYS HELPFUL."

Have you seen soap operas where a guy is screaming or a woman is slamming the door? Somehow, expressing anger has become another fabrication about anger. The work of Tavris (1989) clearly disproves the idea that venting or releasing anger makes things better; in fact, it's the opposite. Tavris's research demonstrates that venting anger simply makes you more upset. If you talk repeatedly to different people about what makes you upset, or call different friends to tell them how bad others are, those behaviors just amplify your feelings of anger.

It's important to notice if you're getting caught by anger in a given moment. Anger is only constructive when you can step back, look at the source of your feelings without blaming yourself, the situation, or the people involved in it, and check carefully what your angry feeling is trying to communicate to you. What's the purpose of anger showing up to you as it did? Anger, as uncomfortable as it is, could show you that you care about something, that a principle has been breached or an expectation has not been fulfilled for you. If you really pay attention to what makes you upset, you will see your hurt, and with your hurt, you will see what really matters.

There is nothing inherently wrong about going for a visit to cranky town; it's about how you decide to respond to it that will really make a difference in your life. You are the only one who can check in with yourself about what's to be learned and then take steps toward acting based on your values.

Souvenirs from Cranky Town

Let's examine a super-sticky situation that occurs when you spend so much time in cranky town that instead of departing it, you buy souvenirs from it.

When you lose it, you lose it!

> It's midnight and after not seeing each other for a while, Anastasia, a super-feeler, and Leonardo find themselves having one of those painful conversations: "I love you," he says, while holding her hands, "but it has been very difficult between us. I think it's better if I move out." Before he even finishes the sentence, Anastasia quickly interrupts him, and with a tone and a volume that is almost screaming she says, "That's it! You want to move out? Go ahead! Who cares what you do? Who cares where you go? You've always been a quitter, a loser. I should never have moved in with you. You will always be the same! I'm not going to beg you. I'm not going to say anything. You want out? You got it! You're just a hard person to live with, a person I cannot trust, a quitter, that's who you're. You don't know better."
>
> Leonardo looks at her with wide eyes, lips pressed against each other; he is surprised and shocked at Anastasia's response and doesn't know what to say.

What could have possibly gone through Anastasia's mind that she responded this way? Where did she learn to respond that way when feeling hurt?

It's hard to manage a painful situation when you're angry, hurting, and feeling consumed with an urge to say something mean, or fighting an impulse to disconnect from the person in front of you. Are you ever prepared for it? Quite likely not. For a very sensitive person, this is the worst: to encounter unexpected hurt, out of the blue. It turns on their emotional switch in a fraction of a second, and what comes next is just the outcome: they lash out.

Let's be real: lashing-out behaviors are very powerful because they can be energizing when you're hurting so badly; you feel so engaged and alive that it's hard to stop yourself from reacting. It's like suddenly a wild force possesses you and nothing can stop your behavior, as if you have become a bull that sees red everywhere and keeps fighting: your target is the person in front of you. This is a super-sticky moment. Have you been there? Check for yourself.

Exercise: Lashing-Out Moments Inventory

Humbly recall those lashing-out moments you have had and write them down, as if you're making an inventory of them. Anastasia, for example, came up with the following list:

- Screaming at her mother and calling her names for not supporting her in a job search.
- Accusing her boyfriend Leonardo of cheating on her after finding out he was still in contact with his ex-girlfriend.
- Yelling at her friend for hanging out with a common friend who she felt had betrayed her.

Going back in time and recognizing those uncomfortable lashing-out moments will allow you to answer the next question: were you in charge of your behavior or was your emotional machinery running the show?

As a super-feeler you're vulnerable to having a speedy emotional switch that goes on and off, and on top of that your body can also go into a high state of reactivity, making it very challenging for you to adjust your response. I call these moments super-sticky moments, because your body is in a complex physiological state that makes everything difficult for you. For example, after Anastasia remembered her "lashing-out moments," she checked in with herself, and realized that she didn't know at which point she lost it; all that she remembered was that her body was boiling all over as if she were standing next to a heater.

When emotional regulation problems arise, people are trapped by extremely overwhelming feelings that go in all directions, and it's easy to go from cranky town to lashing-out land.

Lashing-Out Land

As a super-feeler reading this book, understanding your biological predisposition gives you a frame for understanding those super-sticky moments. Here is one biological marker: according to Gottman (2007), men's bodies tend to have a lower physiological tolerance to stress.

Men react to stress quickly and with faster heartbeats than women's bodies do. Why? Because, through social evolution, our ancestors had clearly defined gender roles: men were in charge of neutralizing all types of threats for the group from enemies, predators, or poor weather conditions, so their bodies were ready to go into fight-or-flight mode at a fast pace. In contrast, women primarily had caretaking responsibilities and developed an advanced physiological predisposition for soothing, calming, and comforting behaviors. Basically, the division of roles between men and women in early societies and repeated over thousands of years helped shape our physiology and sheds light on why men seem more vulnerable to reaching higher levels of physical arousal than women do. If you're a guy, watch out for those super-sticky moments!

Lashing-out moments are like walking through a field of landmines for you and the person you're lashing out at; if you're lucky, the other person may step back from the situation, but they could also respond with extreme anger. Flying off the handle opens the door to the possibility of being hurt and hurting the person in front of you.

So what can you do? Do you recognize when you're losing it? Can you catch yourself when your emotional switch is turning on? If not, here is the first step: get to know your body!

Core Skill: Simple Body Scan

We all respond differently to the challenges of our daily life, and as simple as it sounds, learning about your body will give you the cues you need to catch yourself before a tidal wave of anger crashes on you. A quick scan from the top of your head to the bottom of your toes is a skill to practice and will allow you to notice all the signals your body is sending; you can even mentally divide your body into three areas: head and neck, torso and arms, and legs and feet. When scanning your body, notice subtle changes in your temperature and the tension in your head, neck, and shoulders. If you find yourself having judgment thoughts toward the situation or the other person, those are also cues about your state of physiological arousal.

Core Skill: Grounding Yourself

After checking your body and noticing your body noise, whatever the noise is, press your feet against the floor as a way to anchor yourself, or slow your breathing. Next, see if you can describe your feelings for what they are, whatever they are.

If you are telling yourself things like, "I shouldn't be feeling this way," "Is this the right feeling?" "What's wrong with him?" then you're using an insurmountable amount of brain supplies, which actually exhausts your mental capacities and makes you more vulnerable to being at the mercy of emotions in the heat of the moment. Sitting with an emotion like anger is actually more efficient than fighting it or talking yourself out of it because you're using fewer mental resources, and it helps your body go back to an emotional baseline level more quickly.

Here is a recap of all the steps: 1) notice your body noise, 2) ground yourself, 3) notice and name your emotions, 4) check your values, 5) check the workability of your action-urges, and 6) choose your behavior.

As with any other skill you're learning in this book, these steps need to be rehearsed as much as possible; you can start right now, right here (as my colleague says, don't start practicing a skill when the house is on fire). Setting a daily alarm at any time could be your cue to go through all the steps.

Chapter 11: Isolation City

The emotional machinery is a complex one and it comes with many variations of feelings in pace, intensity, and quality.

There are emotions, such as shame and guilt, that, when activated, make you want to hide, shrink, disappear, or start living like a hermit. It's tough to be in your shoes when these feelings do their best to crush, squeeze, or squash you; yet, learning about these overpowering emotions without running away from them is a core skill on this course on emotion strategy.

Core Skill: Dealing with Overpowering Emotions

Let's start by going over two other emotions that, left to their own devices, will send you into orbit: guilt and shame.

Most people confuse the feelings of guilt and shame, so here is a key distinction: guilt is an uncomfortable emotion about a particular behavior, such as spilling water on the recently cleaned hardwood floor (as I just did), and shame is a distressful feeling you have about yourself as a person — not just in reference to a behavior — but as if something is fundamentally wrong with you. When feeling shame, your mind comes up with labels about *you as a person*: "I'm too needy," "I'm very bad," or

"I'm emotionally fragile," to name a few. Do you see the difference?

Let's take a look at how guilt and shame organize your behavior when they get started.

GUILT: IT'S MY FAULT

Guilt has been called a social emotion because it usually gets started in the context of our relationships with others. Because of that, the experience of guilt could be more pronounced within certain cultural groups in which individuals are more dependent on each other, like the Latino or Chinese cultures. For instance, not spending Christmas or a birthday with your father in a Latin family could start a sense of guilt; the same situation in a Nordic country may trigger a completely different emotion.

Exercise: Taking Stock of Guilt

See if you can recollect key moments when you were consumed by guilt. Take a careful look at them and complete the following chart.

Situation	Body Sensations	Thoughts, Images, Memories	Behavior

Here is the key question for every situation you focus on: did your behavior move you toward or away from your values?

Within ACT, we don't look at guilt or any other emotion as good or bad necessarily. As a super-feeler, you feel what you feel; it is your behavior that counts as effective or not when it takes you closer to or further away from your personal values.

SHAME: SOMETHING IS BROKEN WITH ME

As agonizing, distressing, and uncomfortable as it feels, shame is another emotion that helped prehistoric man sustain the tribe because it established social norms about how to be within a given group; because of its nature, some researchers of affective science categorize shame as both a social emotion and a moral emotion.

Within certain cultures — in particular, Western ones — there is a strong narrative that an ideal person is defined not in relationship with others, but in comparison to others; this explains how shame is elicited by one's own perception of not being the ideal self in comparison to other members of the group. For instance, a client of mine, despite all his successes, when thinking about his family life, felt ashamed because he compared his accomplishments with his brothers', even though his brothers never made a comment or gesture about it. My client felt ashamed because there was an ideal persona within his family that, in his perception, he didn't reach.

In the world of highly sensitive people, shame is one of those secret and private emotions that, when activated, generally starts a string of emotions from loneliness to disconnection and everything in between; as one of my clients said, "It's as if I'm walking on the street, covering my face with everything I can, because without my mask, people will see how shameful I feel about myself and the ugliness I carry within me." Shame hurts.

Shame has its purpose, like every emotion, and the adaptiveness of it can only be understood within a situation. Let's step back and learn how shame shows up in your life.

Exercise: Looking at Shame

Read the directions below, record them with a soft tone of voice on any device, and listen to them. It will probably take you fifteen minutes to complete this exercise at a reasonable pace.

Find a comfortable position, either sitting down or standing up, but allow your body to be relaxed. Close your eyes and slowly direct your awareness to your breathing. Allow yourself to notice every breath you take as you breathe in and breathe out. With every inhalation and exhalation, give yourself a chance to be present in this moment to the best you can be while focusing on your breathing.

Now imagine one of those moments when you were hurting so badly that you just wanted to hide from others. You wanted to disappear, vanish, or fade away. See if you can bring to mind the specifics of that memory in which your inner voice came with self-critical thoughts such as "It's your fault," "Something is wrong with you," or "You're broken." See if you can make this scene as vivid as possible, and do your best to feel as if it were happening in this moment. Notice the different types of words and phrases accompanying this image and, as they come, call them by their name: "thoughts."

Slowly and gently switch the focus of your attention from your thoughts to your physical sensations. See if you can slowly scan your body from top to bottom and notice any area filled with discomfort as a reaction to the memory, and as you did with your thoughts, name those sensations as they show up by saying, "Here is a sensation."

Next, slowly start noticing any other emotions that are showing this moment and bring your awareness to those feelings. As you did with your thoughts and sensations, name those feelings, one by one, by saying their name silently to yourself. Give yourself a chance to allow those emotions to be there. Let them have their space, and allow them to be.

Notice any urges to fight these feelings, get rid of them, or distract yourself from them. Breathe, and kindly go back to noticing and naming thoughts, sensations, feelings, and urges as they come. Notice the emotion of shame. You can even imagine stepping back while watching these feelings come and go, and as you do this, remember to breathe.

Finally, take a couple of breaths and slowly allow yourself to come back into the room.

Any reactions? Learning to pause, step back, and watch these very painful emotions takes courage, and it is a skill to develop and practice. It may feel challenging in the moment, but the more you do it, the more in charge of your life you will be instead of allowing the emotions to run the show.

Because shame is one of those quiet feelings, here are some ways to recognize it in your daily life: notice when you start avoiding eye contact, your speech gets slow, your shoulders are slumped, your eyes look down, and there is a laundry list of thoughts about something being wrong with you. Next, check your values and see if those behaviors are a move toward or away from your values.

The emotional machinery is complex, and sometimes while you're dripping with certain feelings, they could be masking shame; anger, for example, at times can be the second destination of shame. Let's take a look at what I mean by that.

Core Skill: Peeling Back Anger

Have you ever gotten so mad at someone that all you do for hours and hours was focus on how they wronged you, how much they hurt you, or how much they offended you? Your mind comes up with hundreds of blaming thoughts toward others, because it seems that it's all their fault.

I want to give you a clue about these instances — it's possible that in those moments when you're boiling with anger, shame is hidden under it.

Let's step back and learn from one of those moments you were in cranky town.

> *Brian, a super-feeler, decided to invite Tom to his house for dinner. He was excited to make a meal for his classmate, and this was the first time that Tom was visiting Brian at his new apartment. Tom arrived on time, and after Brian gave him a quick tour of the new apartment, he couldn't stop noticing the white pillows with brown dots, so he said, "Brian, those pillows are so mid-century looking. I didn't realize how much you love brown; it's all over."*
>
> *Brian quickly replied, "What's wrong with that? What do you mean by that?" Tom repeated himself, but Brian was trapped by*

the thought that it was "so disrespectful of him, to come to my place and criticize me, just like that. So rude of Tom. I should have known better and not invited him."

Brian was certainly upset and angry that Tom made that comment; he quickly felt a rush in his body as a sign of being upset. That was a crucial moment that peels away Brian's angry reaction and shows what was underneath: when I asked Brian why it hurt so badly when Tom made that remark, Brian paused and responded that Tom criticized him to his face. When I asked Brian again what hurt so badly about Tom criticizing him, Brian paused and then responded that his longtime friend shouldn't criticize him, and also that it was as if there were something wrong with him for liking the color brown and mid-century decor. By checking with himself why he got upset and peeling away his anger, Brian saw that he had a rule along the lines of *longtime friends shouldn't criticize me* — and in one way, that rule protects him from feeling ashamed, that something is wrong with him.

Here is the take-home message and cues to pay attention to when anger is masking other feelings, such as shame, sadness about seeing yourself as broken or defective, or any other type of narrative your mind comes up with:

- When you find yourself dwelling over and over on how people have wronged you, and your mind, like a car pressing the accelerator, comes up with blaming thoughts toward others, that's a time to peel back your anger and look underneath it.
- When you begin to practice peeling back your anger as a skill, see if you can ask yourself the question: Why does it hurt so much? Ask yourself this not only once, but multiple times. When

answering this question, see if there is any narrative about yourself emerging as defective, flawed, or not good enough that the angry feeling and the blaming thoughts are covering up.

Guilt and shame have been studied by different emotion researchers, and while these emotions are hard to have and sit with, they also have a purpose and serve our daily functioning. As a super-feeler, you have a task: to carefully and with intention pay attention to them and see what their function and impact are in a given moment: As with other emotions, notice and name them, then step back and check whether you are acting based on those feelings. Will those actions help you be closer to or further away from your values?

Let's continue our study of the emotional machinery.

Chapter 12: The Emotional Trilogy

The more you learn about the emotional machinery, the more manageable it gets. I like to break down emotions into three categories.

The first category comprises fleeting emotions that come and go, like leaves traveling with the wind; sometimes you see them coming, sometimes you don't. The second category includes other feelings that are more distressful because they're uncomfortable, hard to sit with, and demand you pay attention to them. The last category contains emotions that get your attention because they're repetitive, forceful, and hurt in a different way; they come with a very convincing narrative about who you are as a person.

Core Skill: Dealing with Chronic Crushing Emotions

In this chapter you'll learn about this last type of emotions: the chronic, crushing, and never-ending feelings that seem to bring with them the absolute truth of who you are in this world. The following are the most common chronic emotions super-feelers battle with.

ABANDONMENT

From an early age, Andrea, a super-feeler, witnessed how her parents argued back and forth hundreds of times; she recalled many memories in which her mom would leave their home for days, and Andrea never knew when she would return. At school, when teachers or other kids asked about her mom, Andrea used to respond, "She got busy with work." Andrea recalls how she cried often and asked her mom not to leave, but her mom couldn't stop herself.

In her early twenties, Andrea found herself dreading saying good-bye to the people she felt connected with, like friends, romantic partners, and relatives; in her words, it was like that every time she finished being at a gathering with the people she truly cared about — in the moment they were saying goodbye she had this unique sharp feeling in her stomach as if someone were pressing it and her inner voice quickly said, "They won't come back, they will leave you anyway." Andrea found herself crying for hours at times or doing what she could to hide her tears when going to work after one of those occasions.

Is this familiar to you? Andrea craved what everybody wants: companionship and partnership, but she was continually petrified about people abruptly leaving her. This chronic feeling of abandonment was very present in her daily life; Andrea dreaded it every time she noticed its presence, and yet it was hard for her not to be overwhelmed by it.

REJECTION

Here is another chronic emotion that super-feelers struggle with: the sense of rejection.

> *Jeffrey, a super-feeler, grew up in a blended family that on paper looked like the model family; what people didn't know was that behind closed doors, Jeffrey was perceived by his stepdad and half-siblings as different from everyone else because he was his mom's favorite. Whenever Jeffrey had a fight with his brothers, as kids do from time to time, he would voice his take on what happened, and his stepdad would quickly respond that he was just a different kid and that other kids didn't grumble about the things he complained about. Jeffrey learned to be quiet and couldn't understand why his stepdad said those things, but the older he got, the more frequently he heard variations of how different he was from others because of his height, looks, interests, taste in books and movies, people he hung out with, and trips he wanted to take. He learned to manage all those encounters in which he was being teased, criticized, or questioned by his relatives by quieting down and minimizing how much he spoke. In Jeffrey's words, "I learned to hide myself by not sharing what was I thinking, how I saw things, and what was hurting me. I thought I would be mocked, censured, or simply told that whatever I was thinking was wrong."*

As a super-feeler, the older Jeffrey got, the more attuned he became to receiving feedback from others. It was like his amygdala had a disapproval detector scanning for any comment or gesture that could be a criticism. For instance, when his girlfriend, Sue, asked why he had chosen gray over black for his sofa, he got triggered, and he felt the same feeling he had when interacting with his family as a kid. He experienced a tingling sensation in his chest and his mind quickly came up with the thought, "What's wrong with me for choosing gray for a sofa?" As when he was a kid, Jeffrey would simply look down and not answer the question, but he would then spend hours dwelling on why Sue would criticize him like that when she should know that he loves the color gray.

LONELINESS

Maurice, a super-feeler, used to wake up in the middle of the night with a very pronounced, sharp pain and a cascade of thoughts like "I'll always be alone. There is nobody for me. It's my destiny to be on my own."

> The nights are the worst. Living in loneliness is terrifying at night, in the silence. Loneliness is like a predator that doesn't step back; it doesn't stop until you're in misery and without hope. It's hard to contain; it's a creature that is hard to tame. Sometimes I don't have a choice except to surrender to the wolves of loneliness and emptiness and become a Steppenwolf. The pain of knowing that there is nobody there for you is bigger than you. There is no place to hide. Your misery fills the room and then suddenly you feel the tears on your face. Those tears are familiar to you; you don't want anyone to see your struggle. It's your secret, so you hide your pain as best you can. It's better to be alone, you tell yourself. It's better to let the wolves of loneliness and emptiness take your body and your mind with them. No need to rush. No need to hide. No need to do anything, except surrender. Let the pain come, let the pain take over the moment."

After so many ruptures with boyfriends and close friends, and long breaks in the relationship with his parents, Maurice battles with his strong desire to have a group of friends, people to spend holidays with, friends to travel with, or coworkers to go to happy hour with on Friday evenings. Maurice pays close attention to how people respond to him when he asks them to go out; if a person says, "I can't go tonight because I have to take care of my kid," he quickly detects the sharp pain and it's almost impossible for him not to go into a place of *proving* to himself that he will end up alone the older he gets; his mind comes up with all types of accounts and descriptions about his future as a lonely man.

Andrea, Jeffrey, and Maurice have been battling these chronic emotions that are so painful, hard to contain, hard to sit with, and ultimately, hard to live with.

These deep feelings of abandonment, rejection, and loneliness steal you from wherever you are or whomever you're with; they inundate your body with painful sensations. Whether they're focalized or not, moving or not, or lasting seconds or hours, they hurt. These repetitive feelings carry with them loud narratives, images, and memories about who you are that amplify your distress and make it feel unbearable.

SPECIAL PACKAGING

These chronic emotions come with a special packaging that includes five specific and unique qualities that get them going when your emotional switch is on:

- *They're spreadable like butter:* You experience them in different areas of your life, but in particular, when you're getting close to a person or you care about someone.
- *They're historical like an antique:* You have experienced them from a very young age, at different times in your life, not just currently.

- *They're defiant like a wrestler:* They fight for survival because throughout your life you have relied on go-to tactics to handle them, and these tactics actually make them stronger.
- *They're painful like a sting*: These emotions come with unbearable amounts of pain.
- *They're deceivers like a con artist:* They trick you with a strong narrative about who you are as if they really define you.

Now that you know the qualities of the emotional trilogy, let's look at them in your life history.

Exercise: History of My Emotional Trilogy

Grab a piece of paper and draw a line across it. Imagine for a second that the line is the history of one of these chronic feelings, and see if you can recall different memories of it throughout your life since your childhood. Think about the feeling in your adolescence and young adulthood, up to this moment. Write one word about each one of these memories below the line, and then on top, write down your behaviors associated with it.

What did you notice? Are there similar or different ways you handled this emotion? Do you use quick fixes, like drinking, shopping, or acting out sexually? The more you learn about these chronic feelings, the more you will be able to step back and choose your behavior when they show up.

Exercise: Studying the Emotional Trilogy

For this exercise, find a quiet place and have a piece of paper and pen ready. Read all the directions before you start, and record them on any device you choose. Throughout this exercise, you will be going back and forth between focusing on a particular memory and then writing your reactions to it, so be prepared.

Find a comfortable position for yourself. Close your eyes if that feels comfortable, and if not, simply focus your attention on a single point in the room. Slowly focus your attention on your breathing, noticing when you're breathing in and breathing out. See if you can bring to mind a moment in which you struggled with one of these chronic and crushing feelings of abandonment, rejection, or loneliness as a kid. Just choose one of them to focus on for this exercise, and don't worry if it's the "right" memory. Just do your best to bring it to mind as vividly as possible.

Hold on to this image for a couple of moments: notice the details of it, and even relive it as if it were happening right now. Do your best to stay present with it.

Slowly and gently open your eyes, and let this image fade from your mind. Jot down any reactions you had. Write down the thoughts, bodily sensations, go-to reactions you had about yourself, and the feelings that came with this childhood image.

Then, close your eyes again, bring your awareness back to your breathing, and notice the passing sensations of the air as you inhale and exhale. See if you can recall a tricky moment in your teenage years when you experienced one of these chronic feelings. As you did with the first memory, notice it as clearly as possible; examine the uniqueness of it as best you can. While holding on to this image, notice the feelings, urges, bodily sensations, words, sentences, and thoughts you were having about yourself in that moment. Did you have any criticizing or judgmental thoughts? What narrative about yourself came up?

Let it go, slowly open your eyes, and write down the reactions that came up for you.

Close your eyes one last time, press your feet against the floor as though they were the trunk of a tree, and slowly shift your attention to your breathing one more time, allowing yourself to be present in this moment. Stay with your breathing for a couple of moments, and then see if for this last part of the exercise you can recall a moment in your twenties when you were, once again, encountering the distress of going through these unceasing and repetitive feelings. As you did with the other memories, do your best to bring this image into your mind as vividly as possible, paying attention to the uniqueness of it and holding on to it for a couple of moments. Gently, and while still focusing on this image, see if you can notice what shows up under your skin in this moment. How did you think about yourself?

Take a final look at your reactions, take a deep and slow breath, let go of this memory, open your eyes, and write down any reactions that came up for you during this last part of the exercise.

Now look at your notes and answer the following questions:

■ What type of body noise did you notice?

- **What thoughts or narratives did you notice about yourself?**
- **What impulses or urges came along with those chronic feelings?**
- **How was it for you to go back in time to those memories of struggling with these chronic and crushing feelings, and simply have them, rather than take action on them?**

Stepping back and learning to have these chronic feelings of abandonment, rejection, or loneliness, just as they are, is a core skill because it fosters your capacity to choose your actions. The more you do it, the better it gets, and the closer you will be to being the best version of yourself.

What Do You Do with These Feelings?

Every skill you're learning in this book ties together. Here is a step-by-step formula for you to put in practice when encountering these chronic emotions:

1. Notice them
2. Name them
3. Check with your values
4. Check the workability of your action-urges
5. Choose your behavior

For instance, Maurice, who struggles with high emotional sensitivity, has realized that wherever he goes, feelings of rejection and loneliness come with him. He learned to step back and notice a strong, sharp sensation in his chest along with sentences like, "I won't fit in; I don't ever fit in," and strong urges to stop going to work, stay in bed, and do nothing. Maurice named those feelings as the "classic, old, rejecting ones."

Dear super-feeler, you're not broken and you're not an island; you're just highly sensitive because of your limbic system, your temperament, and your learning history. It's courageous to be in your shoes and face what you face when your emotional machinery is turned on; your chronic emotions, as overwhelming as they are, don't define you, just as the veteran who walks down the street is not defined because he perceives danger wherever he looks; it just happens.

Living the life that you want to live is possible, and practicing, one by one, the skills you're learning in this book will help; over the years, I've witnessed the challenges of super-feelers from young kids to adults, and can tell you that with patience, consistency, and commitment to yourself, things get better.

Chapter 13: The Choice to Feel

Suppose you and I are having a conversation, and you are given two choices:

Option A: You never have to have these awful feelings of abandonment, loneliness, guilt, disappointment, or other overwhelming feelings, but you will also lose your capacity to feel love, caring, and joy with others. You won't feel emotional pain and you also won't feel connection with others.

Option B: You have all the capacity to feel love for the people around you, care for the things that matter to you, and feel joy for small things in life, and you also have the capacity to feel the pain that comes with struggles, frustrations, and challenges of daily living. You live the life you want to live, with both the sweet and the sour.

Which option do you choose? Would you be willing to drop the struggle and let those feelings be?

Every time you fight against those uncomfortable emotions by distracting, suppressing, or running away from them, you spend all your energy in that battle, and at the end of the day, you end up with less energy to do what truly matters to you. What are you going to choose?

Emotional machinery is knotty, and as a super-feeler, those emotions move you in all types of directions and organize your behavior. Although it's hard, it's not impossible to step back, learn to have all your emotions — the fleeting ones, the overwhelming ones, and the brutally chronic ones — and still check your values, evaluate the workability of your action-urges, and choose your behavior.

Imagine for a second, if you weren't spending all your time dealing with your emotions, what would you be doing? What places, activities, hobbies, and challenges would you approach instead of avoiding? What would you start or stop doing for yourself and the people around you? What would you pursue?

Choosing what matters is choosing to feel.

Core Skill: Choosing to Feel

If you don't have control over your emotions, what is left for you? To choose, to learn to have them without becoming them.

Learning to stay present with your emotions is about learning to have your emotions without acting based on them or running away from them. It is about letting your feelings run their own temporary life. It sounds easier said than done, but it's still possible.

In the world of highly sensitive people this is a major sticky moment, because when your emotional switch goes on, those painful emotions are so loud, like the commentators of a soccer game screaming through a microphone, that they demand you take action as soon as possible. And naturally, you may have strong impulses to get rid of them and perform an emotional escapism act by either doing something pleasurable, such as drinking, having sex, eating, or shopping, or simply physically getting out of whatever is triggering the emotion.

Choosing to feel invites you to accept those feelings, as a skill:

Core Skill: Choosing to Accept

You can choose to feel a feeling and yet still notice and name your feelings as if you're angry at them, or you can choose to feel and accept them as they come, with the discomfort, the strong urges, and the body noise they make. You don't have to like or love your feelings, and you don't have to choose to feel them while forcing yourself and gritting your teeth either; you can learn to choose your feelings with acceptance, taking them as they are.

Acceptance is about easing out of the emotional machinery and beginning to stay with what's happening under your skin, right there, wherever you are.

Learning to accept your feelings without becoming them is like being here, in emotion land, before rushing there, to action land.

Exercise: Checking in with Yourself

Set the alarm in your cell phone twice a day to simply check in with yourself about what you're feeling, the intensity of it, and whether it's comfortable or not; if you can't name the feeling, simply describe to yourself the sensations you're noticing in your body in that moment.

The business of being alive is not an easy one, and it certainly comes with all shades of pain, sometimes expected, sometimes unexpected. No human being likes to be in pain, and because you're vulnerable to experiencing your feelings at a maximum level, as if your amygdala were a satellite that captures from the softest to the loudest emotional signal happening around you and within you, you naturally feel as if you have to do something about it right away.

What are you going to choose: to be stepped on by the emotional machinery or to be a super-feeler with a degree in emotion strategy?

Chapter 14: Tying It All Together

Well done! You made it to the end of the longest section in the book. In this section, you have learned very important information about emotional machinery (chapter 5) and the function of emotions in our lives (chapter 6). Learning to chart an emotional strategy course (chapter 7) will help you manage difficult emotions, such as gut feelings that may be emotional noise or emotional indicators about important actions you need to take (chapter 8); overwhelming emotions to pay attention to, including anger, shame, and guilt (chapter 9), because they can drag you into cranky town (chapter 10) or isolation city (chapter 11); and chronic emotions that have been chasing you throughout your life, like abandonment, rejection, or loneliness (chapter 12). In the end, you learned that choosing to feel, even distressing or intense emotions, means choosing what matters to you in life (chapter 13).

You have also learned specific core skills to tame the emotional machinery, including 1) noticing and naming the emotions as they come (fleeting, overwhelming, and chronic ones), 2) checking their function or impact in the moment, 3) checking with your personal values, 4) checking the workability of acting based on the emotion, and 5) choosing your behavior. And sometimes, choosing your behavior is about choosing to feel and choosing to accept your emotional machinery as it comes.

And as challenging as it sounds, there is a difference between living your life suppressing, pushing down, numbing, and wrestling with an emotion, any emotion, versus living a life getting better at feeling whatever there is to be felt. Practicing the above skills is not a one-time deal, but an ongoing invitation for you. Life will naturally bring golden opportunities for you to practice them, over and over.

Here is how Maggie, a super-feeler, handled a situation at work using all the skills she learned in this section.

> *Maggie went to work on Monday, around 9 a.m., an hour before her shift at the nursing facility, because she wanted to be prepared for her next patients, go over their charts, and check their medications. She walked into the administrative office and noticed that the copy machine was not working; without a working copy machine, she knew she wouldn't be able to update the patients' charts as she was hoping to, send faxes to the pharmacies, and distribute different handouts to patients and their relatives. Maggie discovered that she wouldn't be able to prepare for the day as she had planned the whole weekend.*
>
> *Maggie first noticed how her body went into high temperature mode; she also noticed her strong urge to call her supervisor and complain about how the copy machine wasn't working. She wanted to tell her about how she prepared the whole weekend to have a good day, but now she wouldn't be able to do anything, and not only would her week at work be impacted, but also she would have to delay the weekend trip she was planning. Maggie named her feelings as "fed-up feelings," and instead of running to the computer room, she stayed in the copy machine room and noticed how the fed-up feelings were really overwhelming, and how her urges were pulling everything within her to send an*

e-mail or make a phone call. She noticed and described to herself over and over how the fed-up feelings were moving in her body, from her head to her chest, and she thought about a core value of hers: being respectful. She quickly checked in with her mind whether sending an e-mail to her supervisor was consistent with the way she wanted to be remembered or not, and while it was hard, really hard for her, she decided to wait for twenty-four hours before saying or doing anything. Maggie chose waiting as the most workable behavior toward her values.

One last word about these skills: their power lies in their simplicity and how often you put them into practice.

SECTION III

Me and My Inner Voice

Chapter 15: The Birth of Your Inner Voice

When we were born, we learned about the world through our senses; it was a sensing world full of sight, taste, sound, and smell. Then we learned to speak, and with language, everything around us and inside us entered the verbal world; our inner voice was born with this new world.

Your inner voice, like mine, became your constant companion, ready to classify, predict, interpret, imagine, rehash the past, establish cause-effect relationships, create elaborate narratives about anything and everything, and give you advice about what to do and what not to do.

Your inner voice is constantly having an internal chitchat; even in this moment, while you're reading this book, it's organizing these words and connecting them with other similar books, past experiences, and so on. The bottom line is that wherever you go, there is your inner voice; whether you're five, twenty, or seventy years old, your inner voice is there, fully active as if it had a full-time job, 24/7, with no vacations and no holidays. Why is that?

Through evolution, our inner voice is designed to come up with all types of thoughts, hypotheses, comparisons, and associations as a way to organize our internal and external world. From the moment we are born to the moment we die, our inner voice is organizing and classifying, creating hundreds of associations among every single experience we have. Every time there is a new experience, our mind naturally puts all the pieces of the old, new, and current encounters together.

For instance, if I ask you to complete the sentence "Happy birthday . . . ," what does your inner voice say? Quite likely, it will complete it with the words *to you* even if you're not celebrating anybody's birthday today. That's an example of an association your inner voice came up with a long time ago, and guess what? Until your last breath, your inner voice will hold to that association even though you don't want it; it will simply be there. Can you imagine how many relationships your inner voice has come up with?

Your inner voice also comes up with all types of thoughts, and by thoughts I mean not words but images, associations, and memories. Some of them are passing random thoughts, like hummingbirds flying quickly overhead; other times the thoughts are elaborate constructions around a theme or very complex narrative. Still other times, your inner voice comes up with memories or images about past encounters. I could go on, but the point is this: your inner voice is an independent living entity, and it never stops.

Check for yourself how active your inner voice is: close your eyes for a minute and then simply listen to all the chitchat that shows up in your mind; if you have thoughts like "I don't hear anything; there is nothing happening," that's your inner voice, right there. When I completed this exercise, my inner voice told me, "Patricia, you're too distracted with the news, you're not focused. What happened with my sister? Why is the internet too slow? Look at that stain on the hardwood floor. I better get back to this chapter." Did you notice what random thoughts my inner voice came up with? What about yours?

Chocolate and Lemon Together

Sometimes your inner voice is extremely helpful by telling you to take action toward what's truly important to you (e.g., like my inner voice telling me to make sure I write every week to finish this book), protect you from dangerous situations (e.g., telling me to slow down when going downstairs carrying three bags), or even follow rules that are very helpful in daily life (e.g., make sure you pay the parking meter before you get a ticket).

Other times, your inner voice may make things completely worse for yourself, like when telling you to disconnect from others if you're feeling down, rehashing over and over why people have done something upsetting to you, shouting that there is something wrong with you, and all types of things that push you to behave in ways that are far from your values.

> *Camille wants to be in a relationship and feels attracted to Mike; when she sees him her inner voice yells thoughts towards herself like, "Camille, you're too old, you're not attractive, you won't ever find a partner, Mike won't like you." Camille, because of her active inner voice, doesn't talk to Mike and rejects his invitations to go out.*

Can you recall moments in which your inner voice was sweet, kind, and caring, and other times when it was like an enemy within you? If you step back, your inner voice was just doing its job in those moments, as it did with the caveman thousands of years ago.

Your inner voice comes with both: the sweet and sour, the good and the bad, the helpful and unhelpful. It's like chocolate and lemon, all together.

But, why does your inner voice have so much influence on what you do? Because it comes with a hook.

THE HOOK

Are you imagining a hook right now? *The Merriam-Webster Dictionary* defines a hook as a piece of metal or other material, curved or bent back at an angle, for holding or hanging things on. Here is the deal: all that chitchat your inner voice comes up with demands that you obey it and take action; when you do exactly what your inner voice tells you to do, then, as we say within ACT, you're hooked, fused, and trapped by your inner voice.

Is it good or bad to get hooked? It depends. Let's take a look at the impact of getting hooked by your inner voice in your daily life. Grab a piece of paper and draw a vertical line down the page; on the left side write down all the upsides of listening to your inner voice and on the right side, the downsides of it.

After completing this short exercise you may have noticed that getting fused with the creations of your inner voice has a variety of consequences in your daily life. How do you know when getting caught by thoughts is helpful or not? Here is your answer: by checking whether the actions or steps you take, based on your inner voice, move you toward or against your personal values. As you'll recall, workability is the yardstick for a super-feeler receiving training in emotion strategy. If getting hooked in your inner voice drives rigid, narrow, and unhelpful behavior in regard to your values, then it's not helpful to you.

Imagine for a second that you're living your life by doing precisely what your inner voice tells you to do, listening constantly to the stream of words, images, interpretations, or memories that show up in your mind. How would that be in your life? Would you move to Hawaii because your inner voice says that it has great weather? Would you buy every property in foreclosure because your inner voice tells you it's a great deal? It's tricky, right?

Why is this important to you? Because as a super-feeler, when your emotional switch goes on, you can easily and quickly get fused with those fabrications generated by your inner voice. It's like your emotional machinery is a Bluetooth speaker that amplifies those thoughts to a maximum level and then they feed into each other. For instance, when Monica texted her boyfriend Rich and didn't hear back from him in half an hour, she felt very anxious and her inner voice in a fraction of a second generated all types of thoughts: "Is he with another person? Is he replacing me already? I'm just broken, and no one will stay with me," and then she texted Rich multiple times, first with heart emojis, then with texts like "Where are you? I miss you," and then she ended up sending texts with angry emojis.

But wait a minute, you may say, what if Monica's thoughts were true? What if Rich didn't want to date her any longer? Great point. Is a delay in getting back to a text enough to 100 percent believe the thought "Rich doesn't want to date me"? There are many behaviors that could indicate that, but there is a difference between a single behavior versus several.

Monica's inner voice, like yours and mine, spontaneously comes up with hundreds of thoughts. It's like a content generator: it doesn't shut up. But, if you step back, is it really possible that all those thoughts floating in your mind are true or helpful? Quite likely not.

If your inner voice is not a reliable source and you don't want to get fused with unworkable thoughts, what's the alternative for a super-feeler learning emotion strategy skills?

Core Skill: Defusion

Learning to defuse, unhook, detach, or separate from the content your inner voice comes up with is a core skill called defusion. Defusion is not about having a quiet inner voice, or not having an inner voice at all (that's not possible); defusion is about learning to notice the thoughts, memories, images, and strings of words for what they are: thoughts, memories, images, and strings of words, pure content from your inner voice. And remember, within ACT, when looking at thoughts, we don't look at them as positive or negative but as helpful or unhelpful given your values.

Let me clarify some questions you may be pondering:

1. Do you have to practice defusion from everything that shows up in your inner voice?

    No. The key distinction is distinguishing what types of thoughts are helpful to you or not in a given moment in regard to your values. For instance, following with the example of Monica, the thoughts of "Is he cheating on me? Is he going to abandon me?" prompted her to quickly text him multiple times; that behavior was inconsistent with her values of "trusting" in a relationship.

2. Do you have to practice defusion from all negative thoughts?

    No. This is where ACT is very unique and handy; our inner voice comes up with all types of negative thoughts, and we don't have control over what shows up in our mind, just as we don't have control over what randomly shows up on the screen of a computer. As annoying as some thoughts are, the key question is, what's the action you take based on them? Recall chapter 6, when we looked at a situation, the emotional machinery, the behavior, and the consequences. The same type of analysis applies here to your thoughts.

Ready to put defusion into practice? In the next chapters, you'll learn how to defuse from different types of sticky thoughts that most super-feelers struggle with.

Chapter 16: Sticky Thoughts about Emotions

As a super-feeler, your emotions go up and down, left and right, and quite likely your inner voice comes up with all types of interpretations or appraisals about what and how you feel, and then pushes you to get hooked on all those fabrications. Have you been there?

Common Sticky Thoughts

Here are the most common sticky thoughts about feelings that you want to pay attention to:

"I FEEL, THEREFORE IT'S TRUE."

> *I have the truth, period. I know what happened," Peggy, a super-feeler, said, while looking at Timothy straight in the eyes. "You put part of our money in your personal account, then you bought your motorcycle behind my back, pretending it*

was money you saved on your own. How dare you?" Timothy, in a low voice, tried to explain that he did not intentionally put the money in his account; he simply did not realize which account he was transferring a bonus to when completing the transaction online. He said the same thing over and over, but every time he opened his mouth, Peggy said, "Don't you dare lie to me! I know what happened, and nothing is going to change the fact that you do things behind my back. You're a thief and a liar!"

Any reactions? When I discussed this situation with Peggy we discovered that she *felt betrayed and disappointed* when seeing Timothy's bank transaction; her emotional switch went on, her inner voice went to work and organized a narrative to make sense of Peggy's hurts, and she quickly got fused with the sticky thought "I know it's the truth" as well as a story about Timothy being a liar and a person who does things behind her back. When Timothy tried to explain to her what happened, nothing mattered; Peggy was hurt and couldn't separate her inner voice from what was happening in the moment. Her thoughts about her pain and the reality were welded into one, and she was hooked on a sticky thought.

"I FEEL, THEREFORE I AM."

Descartes said, "I think, therefore I am," as if thinking and reasoning were the only proofs of existence and what defines a person. In the world of highly sensitive people, the expression would be, "I feel, therefore I am," as if your whole persona and existence were based on your emotions.

Here is an e-mail I received years ago from one of my clients, Bruce, a super-feeler, requesting that we discuss his concerns about his girlfriend's new job in our next session.

> " *If I tell her that I feel down when I hear about her job, then I'm a downer; if I tell her how scared I am about her going to her new job, I become a fearful man, a weak man. I'm a mess, I'm a downer, a weak person, a fearful person, and what do I do? I do nothing, I just tell her that it's okay she got a new job.*"

Did you notice what happened to Bruce? Based on his feelings, Bruce quickly came up with all sorts of labels about himself. Do you relate to that? Because you *feel* x, does it make *you* x? Bruce was hooked on those sticky thoughts and, as a result, he didn't share with his girlfriend his real feelings; his behavior wasn't an action toward his value of honesty in the relationship.

The challenge with getting hooked on labels about yourself because of a feeling is that feelings are just transitory; they come and go, over and over throughout your day. There are too many to even count them. Imagine if you labeled yourself every time you had a feeling? There wouldn't be enough paper in your journal to write down all those labels throughout your life.

"I FEEL, THEREFORE I ACT."

Mariah asked Maddy, "Are you going to the reception?"
Maddy said, "I'm feeling sad, so I'm not going."

Roberta asked Max, "Are you going to your job interview?"
Max said, "I'm afraid to, so I canceled it."

Did you notice that Maddy and Max's actions were based on their feelings, as if "feeling x" means "doing x."? In the world of highly sensitive people, this is another sticky thought, because super-feelers have difficulty separating their thoughts from their behaviors; they are fused with their thoughts, like Maddy and Max are.

You're going to encounter all types of situations in life, and unavoidably some situations are going to hurt, some more than others; when your emotional machinery is in action, naturally your inner voice will come up with thoughts about your emotions, and, some of those thoughts get attached to the emotion of the moment. As a super-feeler taking a class on emotion strategy, here is something to remember: having a sticky thought based on a feeling doesn't equal reality, doesn't define you as a person, and doesn't have to drive your actions.

Core Skill: Defusing from Sticky Thoughts

So what do you do with those sticky thoughts? You defuse them! Here is a simple and powerful way to defuse from sticky thoughts: notice and name what you're feeling for what it is by saying, "I feel x" or "I'm having the feeling of x." Or you can even say, "Here are my sticky thoughts about my feelings."

Defusing from those sticky thoughts about emotions requires practice, and practicing them daily will teach your brain to step back so you can choose your behavior.

Chapter 17: Creations of Your Inner Voice

Your inner voice is constantly active, 24/7, and comes up with all types of content and interesting creations. Let's take a look at each one of them so you can practice defusion when those memories, images, or words are taking you far away from what matters to you.

Ruling

> *I don't think this is right, period. I don't think she has any right to make any comments about my friends or my family. She needs to drop her comments and just keep them quiet or keep them to herself." That was Matt's response when I asked what really bothered him about Stefani's comment that he's always on the phone with his best friend, Patrick. Matt added, "I have terminated other relationships because people cross lines, and Stefani is just crossing a line when making comments about me and how much or how little I talk on the phone with Patrick; I have to make it very clear to her that I don't have any tolerance for that type of behavior and if she doesn't like it, we can just call it quits, period."*

Matt is hooked on a rule: girlfriends, like Stefani, shouldn't make any comments, especially negative ones, about his friends, family, or anything related to them.

Is it fundamentally wrong that Matt has rules, expectations, or desires about how he wants to be treated or how things should be? Not really.

Since the time we're born we are exposed to all types of directions, guidance, expectations, and rules about everything and anything: don't put your fingers in the outlet; make sure you're back at 6 p.m. for dinner; you're expected to turn in your homework; it's not okay to steal; it's important to pay your bills on time, etc. Following these rules keeps us safe, allows us to be part of a group, and gives us a sense of doing the right thing.

The tricky part is that throughout your life, your inner voice made some or all of those rules your own and created new ones (e.g., how to manage your feelings when getting hurt, or how to avoid getting hurt, etc.), so that you ended up with your own rule book. When the emotional machinery is on, with the speed of a lion you get fused with those rules and take action without checking their workability or the payoffs of your behavior, as Matt did.

Matt was craving a romantic relationship, and for any relationship to grow it is crucial that people can say what they think knowing that they will be heard; when Matt got hooked on the rule of *girlfriends shouldn't make any comment about his friends or his behavior in regard to them*, he deprived the relationship of an opportunity to grow and have the intimacy he would like to have in his romantic life.

How do you recognize when your inner voice goes into ruling mode? Here is a cue: rules usually come in the forms of "ought, should, must, always, or never" to name a few. They also come in the form of rigid beliefs about what's right or wrong, what's expected or not, and absolutist thoughts about how things should be.

Exercise: Identifying Your Inner Rules

This is a short exercise, but it will give you a chance to look into the rules your inner voice has come up with.

Get into a comfortable position, either standing against a wall or sitting down, and for a couple of moments see if you can recall three different memories from your childhood, adolescence, and adult life in which you were hurting and you learned in that situation something about how to manage your emotions, hurts, or what to expect from people. Write down your rules.

Now, answer these questions:
1. What actions do you take when acting based on those rules?
2. What are the benefits of following those rules?
3. What are the costs of following those rules?

For instance, when Anthony completed this exercise he identified the following rules: my anxiety is different than other kids' anxiety; no one listens to me unless I tell them how bad I'm feeling; and people will always fail me. Then, he realized that when getting hooked on the rule "people will always fail me," he doesn't accept invitations from people he doesn't know and doesn't go on dates (actions); he doesn't get hurt or disappointed when people fail him (benefits) but he feels lonely and envious of other people who have a group of friends (costs).

Here is a particular defusion exercise from those ruling thoughts: grab an index card, and on one side write down the three most frequent rules you get hooked on and carry with you throughout the day. See whether you can catch yourself when having one of those rules, and simply check off the rule that got activated.

Learning to pay attention when your inner voice is making rules is a starting point. Let's examine a particular type of rule.

INTERPERSONAL RULES

Nobody likes to get hurt and, unsurprisingly, when there is any possibility about you getting hurt by others, your inner voice rapidly comes up with specific thoughts about how to handle yourself so you won't get hurt, such as "If you really see me, you will hurt me" or "If I tell you how much I care for you, you will take advantage of me."

Are these thoughts familiar to you? Are there other thoughts your inner voice comes up with so you won't get disappointed by others? Here is an exercise for you to complete to answer this question.

Exercise: Recognizing Your Interpersonal Rules

Go back in time to a moment when you liked someone or wanted to spend time with that person; it could be a relationship with a colleague, a friend, a relative, or a romantic partner.

Next, bring to mind a particular disagreement with this person as vividly as possible, hold it for a couple of moments, and see whether you can recall the specifics of it. Remember the words that you heard, your gestures, and your body language as well as the other person's words, gestures, and body language. Did your inner voice come up with one of those protective thoughts so you wouldn't get hurt? Let the image go, and complete the chart below.

Situation	Emotion	Inner Voice Rules	Behavior	Did I get closer or further away from my values?

What did you notice when completing this chart?

As you know by now, your inner voice is constantly active and generating all types of thoughts with a single purpose: to protect you from being hurt.

Holding on to interpersonal rules to protect yourself from being hurt by others is completely understandable; who likes to get hurt? Who wouldn't sign up for a pain-free relationship with others? But is it really possible to prevent being hurt, disappointed, or angry with others?

Here is relationship advice 101: we don't have control over how others behave. As much as your inner voice generates hundreds of interpersonal rules to shelter you from being hurt, it's really up to you to check whether taking action on them is moving you toward or away from what matters to you. You will read more about how to handle relationships with others in another section of this book; for now, it's important to acknowledge the different types of rules your inner voice comes up with when your emotional machinery is activated.

Let's move on to another type of creation from your inner voice.

Retelling

> *Nothing is getting better. I tried very hard to move on but when I was in the car first, and then having dinner with Charles, I found myself going over and over how I met Rudolph, our first dates, our first kiss, the first time we had sex. It was a mistake. The next thing I knew, dinner was over and I didn't have a clue how the evening with Charles went."*
>
> — MARGARET, 28, SUPER-FEELER

Do you notice how Margaret's inner voice took her back to a past relationship with Rudolph, and without realizing it, she couldn't be present with Charles, even though she was physically in front of him? Do you ever go through what Margaret went through? Quite likely yes. If you pause for a minute and listen to your inner voice, you may be surprised to notice how much of what it says is about the past, either through memories, comparisons between now and then, or chewing over and over what happened before. It's like your inner voice got stuck in ghost town and keeps bringing ghost thoughts from the past.

You may be wondering why your inner voice goes into retelling mode. Here is the short answer: your inner voice is just doing its job for you, as it did with our ancestors. They needed to keep track of what went wrong when they were attacked by wild animals, entered territories that weren't safe, or got caught in dangerous weather. Going into retelling mode was a survival tactic for our predecessors; what about *thanking your mind* for doing its job the next time it takes you into ghosting mode?

Sometimes you may find it cheerful to go into retelling mode, like when you're looking at old pictures of vacations, reliving sweet memories with people you love, or reminiscing about your first kiss; the challenge is when getting hooked on ghost thoughts takes you away from doing the doing toward your values now.

Ready to practice defusion from a retelling thought?

Exercise: Ghost House

The next time your inner voice is taking you into ghost town, name each ghost (e.g., "trip to France," "first girlfriend," "motorcycle ride," etc.). Imagine you're holding each one of those ghost thoughts by the shoulders, with both hands, and moving it into a very nice two-story ghost house, where each one of the ghost thoughts has a nice comfy bed. From time to time, if they cannot sleep, they gaze at you from the window with their cute ghosting face, or if they're in a cranky mood, they stare at you with a frown.

If you have a history of trauma and your inner voice is showing memories of painful moments you went through in the past, see if you can practice defusion by saying, "I'm having the memory of x." In the next chapters, you will learn more skills for handling the emotions that are associated with trauma, but keep in mind that this is not a book focused on trauma and you're encouraged to read the appendix section for this particular topic.

Labeling

Have you ever noticed how much labeling happens in a grocery store? There are labels about the price, origin of a product, seasonal sales, special ingredients, and even the favorite products of the employees. Your inner voice does exactly the same thing; it labels, codes, organizes, and judges everything from under your skin to the outside world, coming up with all types of labels and judgments: ugly, attractive, good, bad, rich, poor, and so on. It's an endless world of labels, as if your inner voice has a super-duper tagging machine.

To see how automatic labeling is, complete the sentences below.

My hair looks . . . .
My work is . . . .
My car is . . . .
My cell phone . . . .

What did you come up with? When Jose completed this exercise, he wrote:

My hair looks like a mess, like my mom's hair.
My work drives me crazy sometimes.
My car is a Toyota Matrix.
My cell phone takes cool pictures but needs an upgrade.

What did you notice about Jose's responses? His inner voice came up with facts (e.g., "My car is a Toyota Matrix") as well as judgments (e.g., "My hair looks like a mess"). Jose's inner voice, like yours and mine, is equipped to organize, systematize, classify, and judge everything, anywhere, and everywhere; there are no breaks for the labeling task. However, when your emotional machinery is on, it's important to pay attention to some of these labels, not to change them but to check how it works for you when getting fused with them. Here is what to do if you're getting fused with tags.

Core Skill: Noticing Labeling Thoughts

When Rodrigo received a text from Bill canceling their dinner plans, he couldn't stop noticing how his inner voice went into labeling mode and shouted at him a bunch of thoughts about Bill: he's an unreliable person, he doesn't honor his word, he's insensitive and selfish, and on and on. His inner voice was parked in labeling land for the whole afternoon to the point that Rodrigo got a headache, couldn't continue working, left for home early, and ended up texting Bill a very angry message, saying exactly all that got hooked from labeling country. Rodrigo was hurting, and his inner voice just did its job: to label the experience and the person who hurt him.

Here is how "Saying it as it is, or noticing" as a skill would look like for Rodrigo: "I received a text from Bill and my inner voice is having the thought that Bill is unreliable, selfish, and insensitive; I'm feeling a wave of hot temperature in my body from head to toe, and have the strong desire to text him."

Noticing, or saying it as it is, is another defusion practice; the more you practice it, the more you teach your brain to step back and the more you can choose your behavior instead of labeling thoughts running the show.

Forecasting

Do you watch the weather channel or read the weather section in the news? As you know, it's the moment when a journalist reports the news based on meteorological information; they predict the weather conditions. Your inner voice does exactly the same thing: it forecasts the future.

As you may realize by this point, your inner voice is always doing something, nonstop; it doesn't sleep, and it clearly doesn't take siestas like in Latin America. Our ancestors needed to go into forecasting territory and anticipate the future at all times, just in case dangerous animals or enemies might come their way. They needed to be prepared or anxious about what might come next; otherwise, they could die. Forecasting about the future was a survival strategy.

> 66 *When Megan received a rejection letter from an internship site she applied to, she felt down; the next thing she knew, her inner voice quickly went into forecasting mode: "Here is the first rejection, there are many more to come. I won't get an internship, I will have to wait for a year, potentially get a job, postpone my wedding, delay my dream to have a child, and clearly get more student loans." After Megan's inner voice came up with these disaster-forecasting thoughts, she sat down and smoked a package of cigarettes.*

Was getting hooked in forecasting territory helpful to Megan in the short and long term?

I'm not telling you that you shouldn't worry about anything (that wouldn't be helpful, actually), and at times, it's extremely effective to anticipate the future and forecast what could come next, such as when you're buying a house, contemplating a job change, planning your budget in graduate school, and so on. But watch out when your emotional machinery is in action and your inner voice gets busy coming up with negative forecasting thoughts that take you away from the present or effective problem solving toward your values.

You can't stop your mind from coming up with scary thoughts about things that might happen in the future, but you can certainly do your best not to get hooked on them and go into analysis-paralysis instead of doing what matters.

Exercise: The Taxi of the Future

Next time your inner voice shouts forecasting thoughts about something terrible coming, follow these steps:

1. Notice and name the forecasting thoughts. All names are valid; they can be serious or silly, or you can name them using a keyword — it's totally up to you.
2. Imagine that your mind is like a freeway full of taxis moving at different speeds and in different directions, but each one of those taxis has a sign for each one of your forecasting thoughts so you can recognize them: the disastrous romantic life, the Bolivian tragedy about the office space (hope the Greeks don't get offended), or the car accident.
3. Watch out if you are jumping in any of those taxis and getting lost on the forecasting freeway by either taking action on them or trying to talk yourself out of them.

Chapter 18: Narrating

> " Patricia, when did you get your coffee?"
> "Well, I woke up this morning, looked at the sky, saw that it was cloudy and rainy, then looked around, and of course, there's no better time for a coffee."

And that's an example of how our inner voice comes up quickly and naturally with a narrative. Our inner voice is a very sophisticated device: not only does it go into rule making, ghost thinking, labeling, and forecasting modes, but it also goes into narrating mode. (Be aware that the terms *story*, *tale*, *account*, and *narrative* are used interchangeably and that, within ACT, when we refer to *stories*, we're referring to a string of letters, words, and sentences that our inner voice puts together to make sense of our internal and external reality.)

From the moment we develop language, our inner voice effortlessly comes up with hundreds of narrations about every single life experience we have. If you pause right now, you will notice that your inner voice has accounts about trips you took, struggles at school, fights with your parents, and so on, and every story has an emotion associated with it; some stories make you giggle, others make you cry, others make you upset, and others take you into melancholy land.

NARRATIVES ABOUT THE SELF

Naturally, your inner voice has come up with not only stories about life events but also stories about who you are as a person.

Some stories about you are indeed absolute truths and we call them facts; for example, my story of being an immigrant in the United States is a fact. There are other narratives about ourselves that drag us into a lot of pain; for instance, my inner voice screams at me from time to time a narrative along the lines of "I'm the worst daughter ever because I don't remember my mom's birthday every year."

What are the stories your inner voice comes up with about who you are? See if you can do a mental inventory of five personal narratives that are harsh, painful, and hard to sit with (e.g., I'm a loser because . . ., I'm a mess because . . ., I have wasted my life because . . .).

If you have a history of a difficult childhood or have been exposed to traumatic events, your inner voice may come up with painful stories like "It's my fault my parents got divorced," or "It's my fault I got assaulted that morning." When those stories show up, you may go into defending them, or trying to prove them wrong, or even trying to come up with a positive thought to neutralize them. Those stories come with a lot of pain, and you're naturally doing your best to manage them. What's the problem? As distressing as those narratives are, the more you debate them, the more fused you're getting with them. You're unlikely to win that debate because you're debating with a content-generation machine: your inner voice.

I'm not saying that the hurt you go through when having those narratives is not real or that your pain should be minimized; I'm just inviting you to learn to have them for what they are: personal narratives. And as you may know by now, within ACT, everything boils down to workability.

Exercise: How Workable Are Your Stories about Yourself?

Let's take a look at the stories your inner voice comes up with about yourself, the emotion that comes with each one of them, what you do when they show up, and whether your actions are a move toward or against your values.

Story	Emotion	Behavior	Move away from or toward values?

What did you notice when completing this exercise?

In the world of the emotionally sensitive people, looking at yourself through those bossy narratives is more accentuated when you're hurting because the emotional system in your brain is like a speaker amplifying those stories to the point that you get hooked on them. You become hooked with that sticky thought "because I feel *x*, it's the truth" and then, in a fraction of a second, a confirmation bias process starts based on your emotion: reality has to match the emotion that goes along with the bossy narrative.

> ❝ *Tati is fused with the narrative "I'm invisible, no one sees me on the inside, no one really makes the time, they all get distracted with my looks." When her partner, Richard, mentions that he appreciates her aesthetic sense, is curious about her fears, or pays attention to her preferences for macrobiotic food and a complicated gluten-free diet, Tati's story "I'm invisible" views all those behaviors as nonexistent. She quickly dismisses his comments and believes that he's only saying those things in the moment. Tati only knows that during dinner, while looking at Richard, a familiar sense of emptiness comes up for her, and her inner voice quickly retrieves her invisible narrative.*

It's very natural that your inner voice comes up with a personal story of who you are; even when those narratives are painful, that's not what creates misery in your life. Having those stories is already painful, and within ACT we call this "primary pain," but getting trapped by those narratives, seeing everything through the lens of them, and taking action based on them as if they're your boss commanding you adds suffering to your life. It's already painful for Tati to have the story "I'm invisible," but dismissing Richard's behaviors adds even more suffering.

You cannot control your inner voice from generating stories about who you are; as long as you're alive, that's how it's going to be. But you can learn to defuse from those stories if they're not helping you move toward your values. A low-key defusion exercise, which you're already familiar with, is to notice and name your emotions right away. Remember, naming your emotions or the content of your inner voice turns down your overactive amygdala, the area in your brain that is in charge of your emotions.

NARRATIVES ABOUT OTHERS

> Reuben: I had an awful day.
> Dr. Z: That's a bummer, sorry. What made it awful?
> Reuben: I had a terrible conversation with my sister.
> Dr. Z: With Anna?
> Reuben: Yup, my older sister.
> Dr. Z: Can I ask what happened?
> Reuben: Yes, of course you can. My sister and I were talking about Thanksgiving and she's so domineering and infuriating; she constantly tells me what to do and what not to do. I got so frustrated that I just hung up the phone on her.

Clearly, Reuben got frustrated when talking to his sister; he promptly noticed a familiar pressure in his forehead, and next, his inner voice went into narrating mode about who his sister is (bossy, domineering) and told him to disconnect from the conversation as quickly as possible. Later on, Reuben regretted hanging up the phone on his sister, and when we discussed it, he learned that his regret conveyed something of value to him: he did want to have a closer relationship with his sister. Hanging up the phone wasn't a helpful behavior toward connecting with her.

Exercise: How Workable Are Your Stories About Others?

There is no one better than you to check whether the stories you have about others, and the behaviors that come along with them, move you toward your values. As you did in the previous section, do a mental inventory of the narratives your inner voice has about three people you care about, and then look at the workability of your behaviors when those narratives come up. What do you notice?

Story	Emotion	Behavior	Move away from or toward values?

THE GIFT AND THE CURSE OF NARRATING

It's natural for our inner voice to create narratives, stories, chronicles, or reports about ourselves and others. However, these narratives can be very authoritarian and critical, like cartoon characters at times; they snort, roll their eyes, sigh, tell you what to do, and so on. And, if you get hooked on them all the time, then you're trapped, because they will demand immediate attention and swift action.

> " Ryan, a super-feeler, was discussing with his wife his annoyance that she never seemed to want to take their children over to Ryan's parents' house for dinner. He got hooked on a narrative about her being manipulative and getting whatever she wants, whenever she wants, instead of making compromises sometimes. Ryan's wife explained that his parents usually ate dinner quite late, around 8 p.m., and she was concerned about their children getting to bed late and then waking up in a bad mood the following day for school. Ryan was too busy listening to the narration from his inner voice and getting fused with it; then, he abruptly screamed at her, "I'm tired of your manipulations!" In response, his wife screamed back, "I'm tired of your deafness!" The screaming match went on for a couple of hours until they were both exhausted, and dinner that evening was tense and unpleasant.

Was Ryan's behavior helpful or effective? Did becoming hooked and acting based on the narrative about his wife get him what he was hoping for? Ryan felt annoyed because it is important for him that his parents and children know each other. Did his behavior move him toward that value?

A Few Last Words About Defusion

Your inner voice, like mine and everyone else's, naturally goes into ruling, retelling, forecasting, or labeling mode 24/7; it shouts at you all types of thoughts, images, and memories throughout the day. But when your emotional machinery goes on and your inner voice perceives that you're hurting or getting into a distressful situation, it will go into turbo mode and amplify its content-generation services, at no charge. You may have a strong urge to fuse with those thoughts, take them as truth, or talk yourself out of them, but all of those responses will use more resources in your brain, make you feel exhausted, and prolong your struggle.

> *When Alan was having a conversation with his five-year-old son about an upcoming trip, and the little one said, "I love you, Dad, I don't want you to die," Alan felt a deep wave of sadness and fear about dying early. Alan's inner voice went into forecasting mode: it predicted that he might die next year. It also went into narration mode: he saw the story of his funeral, his son growing up alone, and his wife mourning the loss. Later on, after dropping his son off at school, Alan made calls researching life insurance plans (even though he didn't have the financial means to cover that expense).*

Would you say that Alan's behavior was effective in making steps toward his values or not? You may say, wait a minute, Alan is realizing that it is important for him to protect his child, isn't that a value? Here is my response: Do you remember the chapter "Watch Out for Your Gut Feelings!" and how different it is to have a feeling that is punching you intensely and overwhelming you with strong urges versus being in real physical danger that requires you to act quickly? Those intense feelings are, more often than not, emotional noise.

Your inner voice is simply doing its job, as it has been doing it for centuries, and it won't stop. I encourage you to practice all the skills you're learning when your emotional switch is on. Next time you're feeling overwhelmed by your emotions, follow these steps: 1) notice and name the emotion of the moment for what it is and what comes with it; 2) notice whether your inner voice is ruling, ghosting, labeling, or forecasting; 3) step back and check the workability of your action-urges; 4) check in with your values; and then, and only then, 5) choose your behavior. Sometimes, choosing to feel is the best response you can have.

The more you practice these skills, the better it gets. Creating the life you want to have is possible, as long as YOU choose your actions, instead of emotions or your inner voice taking actions for you.

Chapter 19: Tying It All Together

Here we are, at the end of the section about your inner voice; and phew, you made it. Kudos to you. As you have learned, your inner voice comes with both sweet and sour thoughts, and there is no one better than you to check when getting fused with them is helpful or not.

Here is a brief recap: as a super-feeler, your emotional machinery turns on too much, too quickly, and naturally, your inner voice (chapter 15) gets put into motion (not that it's ever taking a vacation in Maui). It comes up with a laundry list of thoughts: sticky thoughts about emotions (chapter 16); and creates rules, retells, labels, and forecasts (chapter 17) and narrates stories about yourself and others (chapter 18).

What's the challenge with this incredible worker of yours? As interesting as the content of your inner voice sounds, exploring every thought, image, and memory that it comes up with will make you a slave to it. Rather than you being in charge of your life, your inner voice will be bossing you around.

Learning about your inner voice is not the same as doing dream analysis; learning about your inner voice is about noticing its content for what it is: a string of letters, words, and sentences. Then it's time to evaluate your action-urges and choose your behavior.

Throughout this section, you learned an incredible skill: defusion. Here is an example of how it can be applied in your daily life. We revisit Maggie from chapter 14.

> Maggie, a super-feeler, is back at work at a nursing facility, after being home sick with a cold. She is disappointed with the amount of money she has to pay in taxes, tired of working at the nursing facility, and upset with a note she just received from the accountant about patients' payments: "Maggie, FYI there is $120 cash in your money box." When Maggie reads the note, her emotional switch turns on, and a rush of frustration flows through her. She reads the note again and her inner voice comes up with thoughts like, "Who does he think he is? He's being passive-aggressive, accusing me of not keeping track of my clients' payments, and now I have to worry about this, and it's already hard to do this work, but dealing with him is just the worst." Maggie feels a strong impulse to walk into the accountant's office and ask him to stop being passive-aggressive and harassing her about minutiae at work.

Maggie pauses, notices, and names her emotions quietly to herself: "I'm feeling frustrated and I hate it." She pauses again, notices how her body feels like it is boiling, and recognizes a particular type of tension in her forehead. Maggie pauses again and asks herself, "What type of thoughts is my inner voice coming up with?" She acknowledges the narrating thoughts about the accountant and, after searching for a name, calls them "Mr. Snappish thoughts." Then Maggie checks the workability of her action-urges; she asks herself, "Would it be helpful to walk into the accountant's office and to scream at him to stop being passive-aggressive?"

Maggie steps back one more time and thinks about her hurt; she realizes that it isn't the note about the money that upset her, *but rather when she receives any kind of direction, feedback, or instruction from others, she takes it as if she has done something wrong, as if she's being criticized as a person, and as if something is wrong with her. Maggie checks in with herself and realizes that it's important for her to learn to work with others and receive all types of feedback, even when she doesn't like what others tell her. Maggie sends a short e-mail to the accountant: "Thanks for verifying the amount of cash; yes, there is $120 cash, and I'm keeping track of other payments that come in cash. Let me know if you have any other questions."*

Noticing and naming, checking the workability of your action-urges, checking your values, and choosing to defuse when there is unhelpful noise from your inner voice are life skills. And remember, you don't practice defusion from every thought that comes into your mind, such as *I need to put gas in my car* or *I need to pay the cell phone bill*, but from the ones that push you to take actions further away from your values.

SECTION IV

Me and My Body

Chapter 20: How Do I Want to Care for Myself?

Question: How are you aware of what happens around you or inside you? How do you know that you're here, right now?

Answer: Your body.

Your body matters, and we both know that; maybe you have already read books, listened to podcasts, or heard from other sources about physical well-being. Yet, you still dismiss, forget, or ignore this information. This chapter is about paying attention to your body, its basic functions, and the role it has in emotional regulation problems.

Here is another important area of your life to step back and figure out: what is the quality you want to embrace when looking at your physical health? Paying attention to this area is also about enhancing your physical well-being.

Identifying Your Health Values

Imagine for a moment that next to you there is a person who really matters to you. It could be a friend, a significant other, a relative, or someone else you truly care about. Imagine how that person looks and dresses, the facial expressions you see so often, and the way that person looks at you. Next, imagine that this person is giving a speech about what is important to you when taking care of your physical health. What would you want that person to say? Which qualities would you want them to mention that matter to you when taking care of your physical health?

When Natalie answered this question, she imagined that her best friend, Tyler, was next to her; then after reflecting on this, she realized that she would like to be remembered as being considerate with her body. What about you? When answering this question, remember that values are not rules, goals, or feelings; your values are about qualities you choose as important to you, and they're verbs because you're constantly living them.

Exercise: Evaluating How Close You Are to Living Your Values

On a piece of paper, draw a vertical line from the top to the bottom; write your value at the top of the page, and then place a mark along the vertical line where you would rank yourself in this moment with regard to that value. Are you taking care of your health the way you really want to? Are you really close? Somewhere close to it? Or are you far, really far from it?

If you're close, kudos to you. If you're far from it, please don't get discouraged. You're reading this book because you want to change something in your life. This is the time to do it; it may not be the perfect time, and your inner voice may be coming up with hundreds of forecasting or narrating thoughts, all at once. And yet, there is never going to be a perfect time.

As a Latin person, I like to say that living our values is what adds spice and flavor to our life; it's not about perfection but about commitment.

Now that you have identified your health values, checked how far or close you are from them, make a list of ten specific actions you could do in the next ten weeks, specifying when, where, and for how long. Following up on Natalie's example, after choosing the value of being physically active, she listed two specific actions: running 30 minutes three times a week and practicing yoga twice a week for 50 minutes each time.

Ready to learn more about how your brain works? Read on.

Chapter 21: How the Brain Responds to Danger

What makes kitties, rabbits, and turtles unique? Here are three noteworthy distinctions: kitties are constantly checking their surroundings, rabbits move at an incredible speed, and of course, turtles are notorious for moving very slowly.

Similarly, there are three brain structures that, although small, are very powerful in maintaining self-preservation in the face of dangerous stimuli: the hypothalamus, the amygdala, and the hippocampus. You may remember the amygdala and the hippocampus from the first section of this book. Now it's time to pay close attention to what these brain areas do and their involvement in the life of a super-feeler.

Because our ancestors needed to survive, our brain has the capacity to anticipate danger and tell us "watch out, something is wrong." The hypothalamus, like a kitty, checks when there is danger and communicates this information to the amygdala; the amygdala in turn acts at the speed of a rabbit to release neurochemicals and mobilize your body for a fight, flight, or freeze response (more on this below). Now, here is where our responses to danger get tricky. After receiving the message from the amygdala, the hippocampus acts like a turtle and, at its own pace, checks with the prefrontal cortex, the area of planning and decision making, whether the danger signal is real or not in that particular moment. Based on the prefrontal cortex's response, your body makes the necessary adjustments for you to respond appropriately to the situation.

That's how the hypothalamus, amygdala, and hippocampus interact together. But what happens to super-feelers when this regulatory process gets started?

Super-feelers have an overactive amygdala that continues screaming and yelling "this is dangerous" to the hippocampus; the hippocampus is a bit slower, and gets much slower because the amygdala doesn't shut off, so it doesn't have a proper chance to check in with the prefrontal cortex about what is really happening and readjust its response. Thus, super-feelers are left at the mercy of the amygdala, and likewise experience emotions very intensely.

Highly sensitive people basically struggle with having a hyperfunctional and hardworking amygdala and an underfunctioning hippocampus. Because of this wiring in your brain, learning to pay attention to your body is a core skill so you can get better at managing your emotional machinery when it's on and trying to dictate your behaviors.

Core Skill: Notice Your Body States

When your emotional machinery gets turned on, before reacting, ask yourself, Am I at my best right now? How do you discern this? By doing a detailed body scan.

- Do you notice any tension in your face, lips, forehead, or neck?
- What is the quality of your breathing: Is it shallow? Fast? Slow? Deep?
- What is the quality of your posture: Are you hunched over? Are your hands curled into fists? Are you rigid? What is the temperature of your body? Are you cold? Hot?

■ What is the quality of your speech: Are you speaking quickly? Stuttering? Getting louder? Softer?

It's extremely important to start practicing "noticing" because it will give you critical information that is unique to you.

When I encouraged a client of mine to practice the skill of noticing her body, she asked, "But don't I have to *do* something when I'm hurting?" Here is my response: Yes! You can do something right away, and sometimes, more often than not, pausing and checking what's going on in your body are the two best things you can do until you figure out a values-based response.

Practicing this skill on a daily basis will help you significantly in the long run and it's a foundational skill for the other skills in this section.

Fight, Flight, or Freeze

Earlier I said that the amygdala releases neurochemicals and mobilizes your body for a fight, flight, or freeze response. Let's learn about each one of these three modes.

AM I IN FIGHT MODE?

When you're in fight mode, your sympathetic nervous system is activated, stress hormones are released in your brain, your heart beats faster, your breathing accelerates, and your muscles get tense.

When you're in fight mode, you're ready to punch, hit, or box whatever is in front of you. If you get easily angry, frustrated, or irritated, then it's easy to go into shark behaviors with others.

AM I IN FLIGHT MODE?

This is a mapping of Percy's life in flight mode:

■ *At work: When his boss gave him feedback about a recent purchase he completed, Percy noticed that suddenly his heart was beating fast and he abruptly left his supervisor's office.*

■ *Commuting to and from work: When taking the train, which went beneath San Francisco Bay, Percy noticed pressure in his chest. His inner voice told him, "This is dangerous, I'm going underwater, I'll be stuck for a while," and then he quickly looked for the next exit to get off the train.*

■ *At the coffee shop: Percy was drinking a delicious cappuccino, and then he noticed how his stomach felt uneasy, like it was tied in knots. His inner voice told him, "This is bad, you're getting very sick." Percy quickly grabbed his stuff and left the coffee shop so he could breathe.*

Percy's amygdala was shouting at him to get out of all those events; he experienced the same physical sensations as someone in fight mode, but he went into a flight, or escape, response.

AM I IN FREEZE MODE?

If the amygdala continues to scream at a maximum level, and you can't fight, you can't flee, and you can't get help, then the dorsal vagal nerve of your parasympathetic nervous system prepares your body to shut down as a survival response. That shutting-down process is called dissociation: your breathing and heart rate slow down, your mouth generates more saliva, you get quiet, and you basically freeze.

Dissociation is a natural, evolutionary response that some super-feelers experience when overactivated; for instance, when Maureen recalled arguments with her husband Tony, she only remembered that after seeing him screaming at her at the beginning of their fight, everything seemed to be in slow motion; she couldn't recall the words she heard, the time of day, or even the beginning of the argument they were having.

If you find that your body is often going into checking-out mode — people even tell you that you did or said things you don't recall — then it's important that you frequently practice the grounding skills covered next.

Core Skill: Brief Grounding Exercise

What do you do when you go into fight, flight, or freeze mode? You ground your body, as you learned in the chapter on cranky town, with two basic practices:

1. Ground yourself by pressing your feet against the floor. It doesn't matter where you are right now — whether you're sitting down or standing up — you can start by pressing your feet into the floor.
2. Slow down your breathing as best you can. You can even place your hand on your stomach and focus your attention on every breath as you breathe in and breathe out.

If you're up for it, you can also try the following grounding exercise. Though a bit longer, this exercise will help you learn how to stay in the moment even when your emotional switch is on.

Exercise: Prolonged "Grounding"

Find a comfortable position and give yourself 10 minutes for this exercise. Read the instructions slowly first, or you can record yourself reading the instructions and then listen to them.

Place your feet flat on the floor, close your eyes or focus on a single point, and take a couple of deep breaths. Notice where you are right now. See if you can notice any smells or sounds in the air. Next, recall a memory of a mild struggle when your emotional machinery got activated and you were hurting. When you have that image in your mind, see if you can notice any reactions to it; pay attention to any thoughts, feelings, sensations, or urges to act that may be showing up for you.

Take a few moments to notice all those micro-experiences and acknowledge them one by one. If you have any impulses or wishful thoughts to hide, run away, or stop the exercise, see if you can acknowledge those thoughts and name them as "thoughts." You don't have to like them or dislike them; they're simply there. Your experience is your experience; it is as it is.

See if in this precise moment, you can press your feet really hard against the floor, then wiggle your toes, press hard again, and stay present with your internal experience. Slowly place your hand on your stomach, and notice every time you breathe in and breathe out.

Notice how it feels to stay present and in contact with whatever emotion is coming your way; notice how it is to stay with any subtle or intense reaction you're having. Notice how it is to stay present with this emotional chain without doing anything but just simply having it. Notice how it feels to feel what you feel and do nothing. Take some time to watch yourself in this moment. Gently take three slow, deep breaths, noticing how it feels to breathe in and out.

See if you can practice this exercise on a daily basis, and remember that what you practice grows; you're teaching your brain to slow down when the emotional machinery gets activated.

If you have a history of trauma and are affected by it on a regular basis, although this book is helpful, it's not a book about trauma. Please see the appendix for more information on trauma.

Another factor that affects how your brain perceives danger and your ability to stay grounded is your attentional style, the topic of the next chapter.

Chapter 22: Attention and Busy Bee Brain

Does your attention shift from topic to topic when talking to others or completing a task? Or can you focus on a single task, zooming into it, even though your neighbor is playing loud music? What would you say your attentional style is?

Attention is the ability to screen out and stay focused on a task at hand; selective or focused attention is a required ability to navigate daily life, because we're constantly bombarded with all types of sounds, lights, gadgets, and so on, which make it harder to zoom in on a task at hand. Selective attention is in action when you concentrate on the conversation with your friend in a loud restaurant or pay attention to the movie you're watching while your dog is running around. Of course, if you're hyperfocused on a task, like me on writing this book, and dismissed a call from your partner, the sound of the kettle boiling, or your kid crying, that's not necessarily helpful.

Although attention has usually been viewed as a cognitive component of thought processes, your emotional machinery has an impact on it. Dr. Richard Davidson, an affective neuroscientist, has established the relationship between attention and the emotional world. At the brain's level, your prefrontal cortex guides your behavior and chooses which internal or external factors to focus on and which to ignore; this regulation of your attention at the level of the brain is fundamental to your performance of daily tasks and your ability to learn different skills. However, when your emotional machinery gets activated, your attention is compromised.

Your Attention Could Be Cheating on You

Believe it or not, as ridiculous as it sounds, your attention actually cheats on you and you don't know it; this cheating process is called affect-biased attention.

For example, if you were struggling with an elevator phobia, you would selectively check whether there is an elevator in an unfamiliar building immediately upon entering it; or if you had a spider phobia, you may be more prone to search for spiders and even confuse an ant for a spider. Why is that? Because in both examples, an emotional switch goes on, you are flooded with fear or anxiety, the amygdala starts bouncing up and down, searching for past memories in your learning history of similar situations and using brain resources that make it hard to direct the focus of your attention. Instead, your attention is directed by the intense feeling of the moment — it checks, scans, and searches for triggers, which, even when not present, are part of your learning history.

Imagine all the times when your emotional switch tricked your attention and you got cheated by it. When the emotional machinery gets activated, it directs your attention to a particular trigger based on the emotional importance of it, and the emotional importance of a trigger is based on your learning history.

EXHAUSTED BRAIN

Being vulnerable to feeling too much, too quickly, means that your

hardworking amygdala is using all your brain's resources, exhausting them to the point that it is difficult at times for you to have sustained attention. A very common complaint I hear from my clients is, "It's hard to focus on things," and "I'm exhausted, my brain is exhausted."
It's natural to get mentally tired at times, but being at the mercy of overwhelming feelings that consume your behavior makes focused attention a much more arduous task.

Your emotional machinery is powerful and has a strong impact on your thought processes; your exhaustion and mental fatigue are not independent from it. Here is simple and powerful advice: if you find yourself multitasking, drop it, and choose one task at a time.

Tips from the Best Free Doctors: Sleep, Exercise, and Diet

Have you ever found yourself searching to get the best deal you can possibly get, such as when you're making a big investment, like buying a house, or getting a ticket to travel for a vacation? Did you search for a bargain? Here is a bargain for you: the best free doctors are Dr. Sleep, Dr. Exercise, and Dr. Diet.

Dr. Sleep recommends you go to bed and wake up at a regular time; lack of sleep is the number one problem that predisposes your body to emotional regulation challenges. A good night's sleep will prevent your body from going into dysregulation mode.

If you're struggling to fall asleep, watch out for the classic hook of "I'm going to try to fall asleep, I'm going to count ships, clouds, or any variation of this pop culture sleeping advice." The more you try to talk yourself into sleeping, the more resources you're using in your brain, the more distraction you're having, and the less you're likely to sleep. Instead, see if you can gently focus on your breathing, relax your body as best you can, and detect the subtle rise and fall of your chest as you inhale and exhale. The more you let your body be, the less struggle you will have, and the quicker your body will reach a state of relaxation, a prerequisite for falling asleep.

Dr. Exercise reminds us that 30 minutes of daily physical activity helps your body function at its optimal level. Exercise facilitates the smooth functioning of all your body systems: endocrine, neurological, and sympathetic and parasympathetic nervous systems. It enables you to be at your best.

Dr. Diet suggests that you pay attention to the way you eat and the nutritional value of your meals; as a super-feeler, your body may actually be consuming more calories because it's exhausted all the time from fighting your emotional machinery. Let's now turn to how you can soothe your body with simple exercises.

Chapter 23: Self-Soothing Land

We are walking stress bodies. As a super-feeler, your emotional switch augments all types of physiological reactions in your body, making it hard to relax. Learning to calm your body is another key competence that will help you handle the challenges that come when those overwhelming emotions try to take over your day. If you practice the skills below, it will get better and better.

Massage Techniques

Even though the techniques below look simple, they're extremely beneficial and handy. Here is the big advantage: you don't need anything extra to implement these soothing skills, and you can use them wherever you go, anytime, anyplace.

Remember, though, that practicing soothing skills is not about getting rid of the emotions, feelings, or sensations you're having; you're not performing an emotional escape act or using a new quick fix. It's about intentionally and with awareness slowing down your body, not to avoid feeling but to get better at feeling without being dragged into the emotions.

HAND MASSAGE

Choose a thumb from one hand and firmly press it against the palm of the other hand, then rotate the movement of your thumb.

NECK MASSAGE

With three fingers of one hand, press on the side of your neck; slide your fingers up and down. Repeat with the other hand and the other side of your neck.

HUG YOURSELF

Give yourself a 20-second hug: cross your arms around your body, and hold them there.

Self-Compassion

You may wonder why self-compassion is part of this chapter on self-soothing, and that's a great question. Paul Gilbert (2009), founder of compassion-focused therapy, identified three different affective systems in our brains, their functions, and how they interact with each other:

1. The drive system is in charge of pursuing and acquiring what we need (or think we need).
2. The threat system is organized around physiological hyperarousal.
3. The soothing system manages distress and promotes bonding.

All these systems get activated and interact constantly through different encounters in our daily life, including the ones when your emotional switch is on; they allow us to go back and forth between our internal and external worlds. No system is better than the other one; their value really depends on the situation and the context in which they're organizing our behavior. For instance, at times the drive system leads us toward adaptive behaviors, like searching for food and shelter; at other times, it may lead us to maladaptive behavior and against our values because we may get hooked on relentlessly pursuing achievements in our career despite our body's health.

As a super-feeler, your brain is prone to overusing the threat system because of your biology, your learning history, and your temperament. And when your emotional machinery gets started, your threat system quickly organizes your behavior to attack or run away from whatever is causing you to feel threatened. It's a natural response; your caveman brain is just doing its job — to protect you — but it doesn't realize that your environment has changed and that you're no longer living in a wild environment.

An overactivation of your threat system doesn't help your body calm down or settle; it does the opposite. It keeps generating stress hormones that heighten the tension in your body and reduces any possibility for you to step back, check in with your values, and choose your behavior.

This is where the soothing system comes in. Practicing compassion activates the affiliation system in your brain, which helps your body feel physiologically soothed and gives you the space you need to pause and step back. In this section, you are learning about self-compassion, which is one element of compassion-focused therapy. Learning to treat yourself with kindness and caring will help you manage a body that goes to its threat system too often, an inner voice that comes with hundreds of criticisms, and a speedy emotional machinery.

I'm not asking you to go into touchy-feely mode, but inviting you to explore a core skill with the added benefits of science behind it.

Exercise: Compassionate Touch

Focus on the purpose, the intention, and the why of your behavior when practicing this exercise.

Whenever you feel stressed, swamped, or flooded, localize in your body that area that senses your stress and simply place your hand on it, breathe in, and breathe out. Acknowledge your hurt, and instead of judging, criticizing, or harshly talking about it, see if you can let it be with kindness.

Stretching Territory

Have you noticed how many hours we spend driving, sitting down, or in the same position throughout the day? It may be more than ten hours a day. It's not a secret that moving more makes us healthier, and different systems in our body benefit from it; yet, the most common reason I hear from my clients for not doing it is "I don't have the time." I get it: it's hard to be fully active given the hundreds of things we have to do — cleaning, working, driving, taking care of children, cooking, etc. Here is my invitation: wherever you are and whatever you're doing right now, keep in mind that taking care of your body is not about doing everything perfectly but about choosing with intention to care for it.

Stretching exercises are soothing in their own right: they force you to slow down and notice your muscles — where they're tight and when they loosen up. Stretching also stimulates deep breathing, and you may notice your shallow breathing slowing down and becoming fuller. The exercises below are self-explanatory; if you have any medical or physical condition that affects your body, choose the ones that seem to be a good fit for you.

HANGING POSE

Stand up, bring your feet together, extend your arms way up past your head, and then stretch your body up as if you're a ballet dancer, then let your head dangle for a couple of moments.

T-POSE

This is a classic yoga posture in Bikram yoga, or hot yoga. Stand up, bring your feet together, lift your arms as if you're reaching for the sky, touch your palms together, take a few breaths, stretch your body upward, and then bend it forward lightly. While extending your body, keep breathing, and make sure your extended arms touch your ears and your elbows are outstretched toward the front. If possible and if you're up for it, choose one of your legs, and extend it backward, lifting it off the floor to stretch it completely as if you're becoming a human T. Continue breathing, while locking the knee of your standing leg and stretching your body. After a couple of moments, switch legs.

If you can't lift your leg, just stretch your body upward as if you're trying to touch the roof.

RUN LIKE FORREST GUMP

Forrest, the main character of the movie *Forrest Gump*, was always running. You don't have to be a Forrest Gump, but if you're up to it, make the commitment: 30 minutes of running or any other physical activity will make a big difference in quieting your overactive emotional machinery.

Chapter 24: Tying It All Together

Our physical health matters, and for super-feelers, it is especially important because going through hundreds of emotional chains on a daily basis makes your body exhausted and prone to stress; it also adds mental fatigue to that already busy mind of yours.

In this section, you learned to recognize your values about your physical health (chapter 20); explored the interaction among the hypothalamus, amygdala, and hippocampus as a kitty, rabbit, and turtle working together to organize your behavior (chapter 21); examined whether your body goes into fight, flight, or freeze mode, and practiced grounding skills to stay in the present moment (chapter 21); discovered the interaction between your brain, attentional capacities, and attentional bias when your emotional machinery gets activated (chapter 22); and learned simple yet powerful, stretching and self-soothing exercises (chapter 23).

Now, it's your turn for doing the doing! Your values are not just beautiful words; they are for living and guiding your behavior at all times. You can choose.

Here is an example of how Maggie, who we met in earlier "Tying It All Together" chapters, used all these skills when looking at her personal health values. Maggie realized that it's extremely important for her to be healthy so she can take care of her grandchildren, but because she was constantly getting upset with people at work, the drivers on the freeway, the neighbor taking out the trash late at night, and a report she was asked to write for the last two weeks, she wasn't sleeping as much as she needed; in fact, she was barely sleeping, barely eating, and naturally she was on edge most of the time. When she arrived at work, as soon as she saw a dirty mug in the sink, her inner voice quickly went into labeling mode about her coworkers, her emotional machinery got activated, she felt angry, her body felt like it was boiling, and the next thing she noticed she was having an overwhelming urge to scream at everybody and call them pigs.

Maggie decided to prioritize her health and set an alarm for the time she was going to go to bed so she could have seven hours of sleep each night for a week, as a starting point; next, arriving to work, she saw the dirty spoons on the countertop and, while her body went into fight mode, Maggie pressed her feet really hard against the floor, wiggled her toes, and checked with herself what was really important to her. Her answer was her health. She pressed her feet really firmly one more time and intentionally slowed her breathing down, and then she chose her behavior: to feel her bodily sensations, feel the urge to scream, and walk toward her cubicle. In her cubicle Maggie gave herself a hug, pressing her fingers against her shoulders a couple of times, placed her hand on her stomach and continued to slow down her breathing, and then set five alarms on her watch, every two hours, so she could check how her body was doing throughout the day and check whether it was in fight, flight, or freeze mode. It wasn't an easy day for Maggie, because her emotional machinery was still on edge, but Maggie didn't regret not screaming at her coworkers, not making faces at them, and not feeling scared that someone would complain about her unprofessional behavior and then she'd lose her job.

Me and the People I Care About

Chapter 25: Relationships Are a Messy Business

As I have said many times, "A life well lived has strong connections with the people we love." We have survived as a species not only because of biological adaptation, but also because of our connections with others. Our ancestors learned very early that in order to survive they required the group, and to be part of the group they needed to learn to foster different types of relationships. We're wired to connect, and building connections with others is one of the most precious things we can do in life; without these connections, we are vulnerable to profound suffering, loneliness, and isolation.

But relationships are not just like flowers and butterflies; they are difficult to look after, maintain, and be in. Most of us go through life using a trial-and-error approach to creating healthy, caring, and fulfilling connections with others. But do we really know what we are doing all the time? Probably not. Creating a relationship from scratch is not an easy project; it's actually a complex undertaking because, as fun as relationships are, we also get hurt. Every time there is a disappointment or rupture, there we are again: covered in visible or invisible tears, trying to pull ourselves together in the midst of the emotional turmoil, and simply surviving from moment to moment. Have you experienced that?

This chapter is about helping you create the relationships you want to have. Here is the first question:

What sort of relationships do you want to build?

Quite likely, at some point, you have thought about the relationships you would like to have and how you would like to be within them. Within ACT, this is a pivotal question and is part of your training on emotion strategy to figure out your interpersonal compass.

Keep in mind that this question is not about what you want to do with others or how you want to be treated; it is about discovering how you want to be within your relationships, regardless of how other people behave around you.

Let's try an exercise to clarify your interpersonal values.

Exercise: Discovering Your Interpersonal Values

Find a comfortable location to be in for 10 to 15 minutes. Sit in a position where you are as comfortable as possible, have a piece of paper and a pen next to you, and read the instructions before practicing the exercise. You can even record it with a soft, slow voice, and then do the exercise while you play back the instructions.

Close your eyes, if possible, and anchor yourself in your breathing. Take a couple of moments to notice your breathing; notice every time you breathe in and breathe out. Then imagine the following scene: You're celebrating your seventieth birthday

with your partner, friends, and relatives. Give yourself a couple of moments to imagine this very important occasion: visualize the place where your birthday gathering takes place, the time of day, the colors that are unique to the scene, and the people gathered there to celebrate you. They're all there. You can see them one by one; you can see all the people who matter to you and who have made a difference in your life. Then imagine them giving a speech about how you were in your relationship with them.

Here is your romantic partner, giving a speech, and you are looking at this partner you were in the relationship with. You listen as your partner slowly talks about your character and the type of partner you were within the romantic relationship. After holding this first scene in mind, slowly go back to your breathing, open your eyes, and write down your response. What did your partner say?

Gently go back to closing your eyes, and anchor yourself one more time in your breathing, noticing each breath as you breathe in and out. Every time you breathe in, do your best to breathe out intentionally slowly. Then, bring your mind back to the image of your seventieth birthday, and after holding this image in mind for a moment, imagine that this time it is your best friend who is getting ready to give a speech about how you were within your friendship. Your friend knows you very well, has a history with you, and has been there with you in both good and bad. Slowly imagine what your friend would say about the qualities that were important to you as friend and the qualities you brought into the friendship. As you did with the other scene with your partner, slowly transition into the room. Take a couple of slow, deep breaths as you open your eyes, and then write down what you heard your friend say to you.

Finally, bring yourself back to your seventieth birthday scene for one last time, and after holding this image in mind for a couple of moments, see if you can visualize a family member who has been a constant presence in your life, one who has been there with you over the years. This relative knows you and sees you on a deep level and now is sharing with others what qualities were important to you as a family member; see if you can imagine what qualities your relative will say you brought into the relationship or what type of family member you have been. Now, for the last time, do your best to listen to those words, and after holding them in your mind for a couple moments, let this image fade, anchor yourself in your breathing, open your eyes, and write down your response.

Read all of your responses, and see the themes that emerge from them: the core qualities that are important to you. You can also add other values that are important to you but may not have shown up in the exercise. These are the qualities you want to hold on to and nurture in your relationships with your romantic partners, your friends, and your family members.

When Ryan completed this exercise, he clearly saw that within his friendships it was important for him to be supportive. In his romantic relationships, he wanted to see others for who they really are, and with his family relationships, he wanted to be a caring relative. When Ryan identified his values in different areas, it showed him a map that he didn't have before. As one of my clients said, "I didn't know that I could choose who I wanted to be in my relationships."

Living Your Interpersonal Values Is Possible, Right Here, Right Now

Living your interpersonal values is not a fantasy movie but a real process. You can start right here, right now, behaving as the person you want to be with the people you care about. There is no need to wait for the ideal conditions; you can begin now to move toward what matters.

For instance, Mauricio, a client struggling with terminal cancer, felt scared while he was preparing to go through the process of chemotherapy. Because of his illness, he was afraid of not being able to be the loving and protecting father he wanted to be with his children. After discussing his fears about the medical treatment and his dread about letting his kids see him get sicker, lose hair, or throw up, Mauricio decided to give them a kiss every day and play for five minutes while going through radiation. Mauricio chose to live his values, even though the circumstances weren't ideal.

Going back to your interpersonal values as your interpersonal GPS is the best compass you have to create fulfilling relationships. The next chapters will help you get there. Keep reading!

Chapter 26: Relating to Relatedness: Attachment Styles

We learn how to relate to others based on our relationships with our parents or caregivers. As cliché as it sounds, there is some truth to it. Fifty years ago, we didn't have science to explain it, but now we do. Neural plasticity of the brain was confirmed in approximately the year 2000; our brain has the biologically innate capacity to grow new neurons and create new synaptic connections, all from new experiences, all from neural firing. Interpersonal neurobiology, pioneered by Dan Siegel at UCLA, is the science of applying the discoveries of neuroscience to different aspects of human relationships: attachment is one of them and is the focus of this chapter.

Attachment has been the topic of many studies from Cassidy and Shaver (2016) to the work of Siegel (1999). Here are the key points to remember:

- We're genetically coded to walk, talk, learn, and perform other functions, and it's in the interaction with others and our surroundings that our brain gets stimulated to continue developing. That's nature.
- When we're born, in the early stages, the right hemisphere in our brain assists us in learning about the world through our senses;

we sense and sense, even though our brain is not fully developed. And we actually store those memories in our brain, in our implicit memory. That's the beginning of our attachment styles.

- When language gets developed we continue to learn about ourselves, others, and the world, but this time, we store those memories explicitly and symbolically.

What's the take-home message? Our relational world gets established from the moment we're born to the moment we die. We sense, and then we remember. We sense how to relate to others, and then we remember how to relate to others.

Why is attachment so important for super-feelers? Here are two core reasons:

1. When you were born, and your body and brain were not fully developed, it was a scary, unstable, and chaotic world and in this sensitive time you learned to self-regulate through the interactions with the people closest to you.

   You may have learned to calm yourself with others when feeling scared or anxious, or you may have learned how it feels to be rejected if your caregivers were not available to you, or you may have learned how confusing and anxiety-provoking it was to sometimes be soothed and other times not.

   Emotional regulation starts through those interactions. As you grow older, you continue to learn to regulate or manage what you experience and feel on your own, but you already have memories of those first encounters.

2. You basically learned to relate to others very early, and that

relational learning repeated itself and created a pattern in your life; it is as if those early experiences gave your inner voice relational rules that guide you in how to be with others.

Attachment Styles

Your attachment style is a variable that plays out in your relationships; it's not a coincidence, but part of your learning history. Let's learn about each attachment style.

ANXIOUS: I WANT TO MAKE SURE YOU REALLY LIKE ME

> *After Sasha had brunch with Robin, her best friend, she left to go study. On her way back home, she wanted to continue chatting with Robin about a date she had had. She called Robin, left a message, and didn't hear back; then she texted her, and didn't hear back; two hours later, she called and texted Robin and still didn't hear back. Every time she either texted or called Robin, she felt this hollow sensation in her throat, and her inner voice quickly said, "Does she really want to be my best friend? Is she talking more with Rebecca right now? Did I say something wrong at brunch? Is it possible she just decided to stop hanging out with me because I'm going to start dating?"*

Sasha is prone to an anxious attachment style.

DISORGANIZED: I WANT YOU AND I DON'T WANT YOU

> 66 *Torin went on a date with Marci. He really liked her, and she liked him too. They agreed on continuing to get to know each other; as soon as they said goodbye to each other, Marci texted Torin, but when he grabbed his phone and saw Marci's name, he suddenly felt a wave of fear, and his inner voice came up with thoughts like, "Maybe this is not real; maybe it's too much right now." He didn't answer the text Marci sent him, or the ones she sent him after that. Hours later, Torin called Marci and behaved as if nothing had happened. He simply told her how much he liked her.*

Torin struggles with a disorganized attachment style, and he usually behaves in very confusing ways to others when he begins to get close to them. He really wants to bond, connect, and belong to a group, but it's anxiety provoking to get close, so sometimes he shows how connected he wants to be, and at other times, he just quickly disconnects, all within the same relationship.

DISMISSIVE: I DON'T WANT TO WANT YOU

> 66 *John is extremely independent and self-sufficient, and on the outside, it's as if he has everything under control. He doesn't need anyone or anybody; he can handle life as it comes on his own. John has a bunch of acquaintances that he spends a lot of time with every week. His calendar is usually full with all types of events, from dinners to gallery nights, and everything in between. John is fun to hang around with and he enjoys his friends, but in the middle of the gathering he looks around and*

sees all his friends with their significant others and when he goes back home, there is an empty apartment waiting for him and no one to share his day with. He feels lonely, deeply lonely, but he minimizes it, and acts as if companionship doesn't matter.

John has a dismissive attachment style.

SECURE: I WANT YOU AND I'M OKAY WANTING YOU

Marissa has moved through different cities as an immigrant; because of her job as a nurse with Doctors Without Borders, an international health organization, she has gone back and forth between Europe and the United States. Marissa just started dating Kevin, a graduate student. Marissa plays volleyball and watches movies with him and is thinking about introducing him to her friends; sometimes, they text each other throughout the day; other times, it's hard because of their occupations. When Marissa doesn't hear back from Kevin, she misses him, sends him an emoji, or waits until he's available. One time Kevin couldn't make it to one of their dates. Marissa got upset and frustrated but when she learned that Kevin couldn't make it because his car broke down and he didn't have a way to call her because of the area's poor reception, she checked to see if there were other times they could get together. Marissa was still upset, curious about Kevin, and didn't radically disconnect from him.

Marissa wants to be in a relationship and feel close to others, and she is comfortable with her full range of emotions. Marissa's style of relating to others is secure.

Which style of relating to others speaks to you: are you most like Sasha, Torin, John, or Marissa? Keep in mind that your style may not fit any particular one to a T, and it may even shift from relationship to relationship.

Overcoming Your Learning History

Relationships are work, without exception, and having a particular relating style makes you vulnerable to automatically forming relationships that take you far away or close to the quality of connections you want to have. Being aware of how you operate in relationships makes you less susceptible to following the pattern your learning history has created and to actually overcome it.

Here is a piece of brain-based information: as Dr. Siegel (1999) stated, "Neurons that fire together, wire together." This simple yet powerful sentence means that any experience you have causes neurons in your brain to fire; repeated experiences cause neurons to fire repeatedly, and that's how new neural pathways develop. Therefore, if you shift your relational behaviors, in particular when your machinery is on, you're creating a new pattern, a new neural pathway in your brain.

No matter how you related to others up to this point, change is possible. Your brain is wired to make radical shifts. But what if people are reacting to you in ways you don't understand? Your nonverbal communication may be playing a role; it's time to examine the ways your posture, facial expressions, and tone of voice may be affecting how you relate to others.

Chapter 27: Nonverbal Communication: Your Body, Posture, Face, and Voice

> 66 *Jessica went to play basketball, and after shooting, dribbling, and passing the ball back and forth with her teammates, she accidentally fell and her body hit the ground on her right arm. A week later, she walked into my office wearing a cast and with a new realization: "I didn't know how much I rely on my arms when greeting, talking to others, or presenting my work in meetings."*

How You Relate to Others

We communicate with our body 24/7 and we forget about it 24/7, too. Our body is at the center of the emotional machinery from the beginning to the end, and yet we overlook, disregard, or forget about it.

As part of your training on emotion strategy, it's important to pay attention to how you're relating to others: Are you present? Are you aware? Let's briefly visit each one of these skills.

PRESENCE

You cannot engage with others unless you're there, fully present — not 5 percent or 10 percent, but 100 percent. Naturally, and as expected, the ongoing chitchat of your inner voice will throw out all types of distractions (e.g., check out the red painting on the wall; that car looks so cool, etc.), and as challenging as it is, focusing on the person you're talking to by intentionally paying attention to what they're saying will help you stay present.

AWARENESS

Have you been in situations where you are concerned about your cell phone bill, decide to call the company, are clear about what you need to say, but then, the next thing you know, you're yelling at the person on the other end of the line? It happens to all us when the emotional machinery runs the show, and because of that, it's important to be aware of how you're relating to others.

Nonverbal Communication

You can be present, but if you're not aware of your nonverbal communication — what your posture, your face, and your tone of voice are saying — then you're not really there. Let's break it down.

YOUR POSTURE

There are hundreds of body postures to discuss, but this is not a Wikipedia article about body language; this is a section to give you the basics so you can communicate effectively.

As you will recall from the section "Me and My Body," your body can go into fight, flight, or freeze mode, and you naturally adopt a particular type of posture, facial expression, and tone of voice for each one of these modes:

- **Fight mode:** Your body is leaning in toward the other person, chest out, chin up.
- **Flight mode:** Your shoulders are lifted, your eyes are wandering, and you may be tapping your foot or fidgeting with your fingers.
- **Freeze mode:** Your shoulders are shrinking, your arms are down, and your face may be looking down.

It's important that you check your body and, if it is in one of these modes, make a conscious decision to calm down by focusing on your breathing, intentionally slowing it down, and pressing your feet really hard against the floor so you can ground yourself.

Now, here is an alternative posture, not a perfect one, but a different one to communicate effectively:

- **Welcoming posture:** Your shoulders are low, your head is lifted, your back is straight but not tight, there is a bit of space between your legs, your arms are not crossed in front of you, and your hands are not stuffed in your pockets.

YOUR FACE

It's important to notice any tension in your face, and in particular any tightness in your forehead or your jaw, as if you are moving your teeth back and forth. Try to relax your facial muscles so you are not scrunching your forehead, gritting your teeth, or squinting your eyes.

YOUR VOICE

Are you speaking quickly or slowly, loudly or softly? Are you enunciating words or do you sound like you're singing in a karaoke bar? Are you pausing? There are four elements to be aware of when studying your voice: rate, volume, pitch, and pauses.

It all depends where you are and who you are, of course. Have you ever watched Tony Robbins, a motivational guru, during his TED Talk? When he's on stage, he waves his arms, jumps up and down, and speaks quickly and loudly. That's very effective for what he is doing: motivating hundreds of people and making sure they pay attention to him. But this won't be appropriate if you are speaking one-on-one with a date in a quiet restaurant. Likewise, when you're playing with children, you might use a chatty, low-key tone of voice.

Every relationship requires adjustments in our body language and tone of voice. It's important to be aware of how you are coming across and project the values you want to move toward in all areas of nonverbal communication. Being aware of your nonverbal communication will also help you avoid unnecessary conflict in relationships, the topic of our next chapter.

Chapter 28: Conflict in Relationships

Conflict in relationships is inevitable and unavoidable. Super-feelers are often very reactive to conflict because it hooks into their emotional machinery and starts a chain of emotions and action-urges. To slow this process down and give you time to examine your values and choose your behaviors, it's important to examine what your inner voice is telling you about conflict and to explore how your family handled conflict, which is part of your learning history. Let's look at the inner voice first.

Your Inner Voice on Conflict

As you know by now, your inner voice comes up with all types of ruling, ghosting, labeling, forecasting, and narrating thoughts about everything, everywhere. Naturally, in relationships, there is going to be conflict, and of course, your inner voice, effortlessly, has come up with thoughts about conflict.

Let's take a look at the most common thoughts about conflict that super-feelers wrestle with.

YOU CHANGE FIRST, THEN I'LL DO IT

> *Richard was having drinks with his friends and just hanging out for happy hour. Andre asked him about how his dating life was going, and after a couple of updates on the people he was seeing, Richard said, "You know how it is, if in a relationship people ask you to change something or they go on and on with the accommodation or adjustment talk, I ask them to change first; they have to show me they can change first, so then I know it's okay to do something different."*

It's hard when people ask us to change and make adjustments or accommodations at any point in any relationship. We all have thoughts about how to handle disagreements with others, and that's natural. Richard's inner voice had the thought "you change first, then I'll do it." The problem with that thought is that you get hooked on it, hold on to it with white knuckles, and do exactly what the thought pushes you to do, without checking whether those actions are helpful to the relationship in a given moment.

THERE ARE WINNERS AND LOSERS

Quite often, super-feelers have been hurt by others in the past and are scared about people hurting them in the future, so their inner voice works overtime to protect them, coming up with this thought: they are winners and losers in a conflict. If super-feelers get hooked with this thought or variations of it, they quickly go into convincing mode, proving they're right and the other person is wrong.

I DON'T WANT TO ARGUE: I WANT TO BE LIKED!

It's understandable you want to be liked, appreciated, and seen in a good light by others. The challenge is that conflict is going to show up, anytime, in any given moment, and it is part of any relationship. Sometimes you may be liked, sometimes you may not be. It's hard to predict and, unfortunately, you don't have control over how others perceive you.

Exercise: Examining Thoughts About Conflict

Are there any other thoughts about conflict you have learned over the years? Write them on a piece of paper, examine the behaviors that come with them, and see if they take you further away from or closer to your interpersonal values. Do they help you have the relationships you want to have, or not?

Conflict Tactics: The Heart of the Problem

We often think of conflict as people screaming at each other, but it's not the only way in which conflict presents; conflict exists anytime two or more people have a clash of opinions, wants, desires, and wishes. For super-feelers, a fight can feel like a combat zone when your emotional machinery is on.

As much as genetic science has evolved, there is no genetic code for how we handle conflict; we learn how to argue by watching the people around us, listening directly to lessons about conflict that people give us, and having hundreds of arguments ourselves as we go through in life.

How do you argue? Do you have your go-to tactics for handling a fight? I call them "go-to tactics" because, if you pay attention, they are actually specific behaviors you do or say in the middle of a fight.

These go-to tactics are familiar to you for a single reason: you use them over and over; you overlearn them to the point that they become second nature when fighting with others.

HOW DID MY FAMILY HANDLE CONFLICT?

A client told me once: "I never understood why, when I'm upset, my wife wants to talk to me; all I wanted was to shut down, disconnect, physically and emotionally; it took me years to realize that I was doing exactly what my father did when arguing with my mom. I became him without noticing and arrogantly believing it was the way to handle conflict." Our repertoire of go-to conflict tactics starts with our upbringing, and no one is exempt from that; we're human beings with a history and not robots coming up from a lab.

Exercise: Going Back in Time

Find a comfortable position and give yourself 10 minutes to complete this exercise. If you feel comfortable, close your eyes, focus intentionally on your breathing, and go back in time to your childhood. See if you can recall a moment in which either your parents or caregivers were arguing. Bring to mind an image as vividly as possible: try to recall their words, body posture, and tone of voice, and see if you can notice the response of each one of the people involved. How did your mother respond to this conflict? What did your father do? Take a couple of moments, holding that memory in your mind, before going back to your breathing. When you are ready, open your eyes. Write down your responses to these two questions:

1. **How did your mother, father, or the person you grew up with handle the conflict?**
2. **What was the outcome for the relationship?**

For instance, Mariah recalled that her mother used to lash out when arguing with others, and most of the time, she couldn't stop herself from blaming, attacking the other person, and then going into "stonewalling mode." Her father, on the other hand, usually relied on stonewalling as his primary go-to tactic when encountering conflict. The outcome for their relationship were days without them talking to each other, her mother screaming and making demeaning comments to her father, and her father ignoring her mother and watching hours of television.

Learning to behave differently involves looking at your learning history; kudos to you for paying attention to the early memos you received about handling conflict. The next step is to look at the go-to tactics you currently rely on when getting hurt and walking into a fight.

Current Go-to Conflict Tactics

Below are the most common go-to tactics that super-feelers use when feeling hurt; some of them may relate to you more than others, or you may have used them all at different times in your life.

FORCEFUL LIKE A HAMMER: DEMANDING, MAKING THREATS

> *I promise you that if you don't let me go out right now, I'm going to let your friends know what type of person you are."*

This was Sean's response to Rebecca when she shared her concerns about his alcohol consumption, dropping out of school, and being unemployed. Sean instantly felt shame and embarrassment, and without thinking twice, he responded to those overwhelming feelings as he had learned to: by making threats so that the other person would stop bothering him.

Going into hammer mode comes with making blunt threats, demands, or unreasonable requests. Sometimes you may yell; other times, you may make a threat with a soft tone of voice.

QUICK LIKE A WHEEL: BLAMING

> *After being in an eight-month relationship and having sweet, caring, loving, and also challenging, rocky moments, Thomas decided to clean the apartment he recently rented with his girlfriend Pam, a super-feeler. He started picking up clothes off the floor, glasses from the coffee table, sport shoes from the entrance door, and dinnerware from Pam's work area. When he turned around, he unexpectedly saw on the large computer screen an e-mail from Pam with the words "love and commitment." He got confused and his eyes couldn't stop gazing at the top of the e-mail; the e-mail was addressed to one of Pam's ex-boyfriends. Thomas was shocked and confused, and nothing made sense for him in that moment. When he confronted Pam, she blushed, grew ashamed, and then said, "We were having such a bad time; everything felt like a mistake after we moved in together. I tried, but you put me in this situation; you smother me and criticize me, it's your fault I ended up contacting my ex."*

Blaming or externalizing go-to tactics make others responsible for your distressful feelings, sensations, and even behaviors.

I'm not saying the things others do aren't wrong or inconsiderate, but blaming them distracts you from noticing your own hurt. When your emotional switch is on, your inner voice quickly comes up with a simple cause-and-effect relationship between your hurt and the other person's behavior when your emotional switch is on. I wish it were as straightforward as that, but it's not. You feel what you feel, and blaming others without looking within is not helpful.

When Pam was confronted by Thomas, she quickly responded with, "It's your fault." But when she checked in with herself, she realized she had been full of shame for hurting Thomas in that way; she was ashamed because she found herself doing what others had done to her before. But when she was confronted, she didn't know any other way to handle her shame at that moment.

LOGICAL LIKE A COMPUTER: REASON GIVEN

> *I have chronic pain, I can't take regular medication, I have anxiety, and now I have trauma because of my family situation; I cannot get a job or go to school. I need money so I can buy my own weed. I deserve to be treated as a young adult in transition."*

This was James's response to his father, Arthur, after he refused to give him his allowance for the week. James had been smoking weed at home on a daily basis, and he even tried street drugs the weekend before. Arthur was worried about James's judgment and safety and believed he needed to monitor his access to money.

James became hurt and upset about being denied his allowance and quickly went into computer mode by giving a hundred of reasons why he should get what he wanted, without learning about or listening to his father's concerns.

Going into computer mode as a go-to tactic is listing all the reasons, explanations, or justifications that your inner voice comes up with in the middle of a fight. What's the outcome? You don't hear the other person and your behavior may be unhelpful for achieving the relationship you want to have. I'm not saying you don't have valid reasons to do what you do, say what you say, or feel what you feel; I'm just inviting you to notice whether holding on with white knuckles to those narratives is effective. Do you get closer to your interpersonal values?

SHARP LIKE A KNIFE: CHARACTER ATTACKS

Criticizing is one of the most damaging behaviors in a relationship. (Be aware that we'll use the terms *criticism*, *character attacks*, and *personality generalizations* interchangeably.) This is what this particular go-to tactic looks like.

> **Peter:** *Sweetie, I told you to please not share with our neighbors our problems because I don't know them well like you do, and I feel uncomfortable with our intimate issues being exposed in that way.*
>
> **Susan:** *Peter, stop being a demanding person and trying to control me by telling me what I can and cannot share with others. It's my friendship, my relationship with them, and if you weren't so sensitive and controlling you wouldn't care. It's your sensitivity crap trying to control us.*

Susan gets annoyed with Peter's request, draws a line around what he can or cannot tell her, and then criticizes him about who he is as a person instead of referring to the specific behavior she doesn't appreciate in the given moment. Susan verbally attacks Peter and his needs, as if it is wrong of him to ask for what he needs and is important to him.

When feeling upset and going into knife mode, your inner voice doesn't distinguish the person from the behavior, and therefore the whole person's character comes under attack rather than a specific behavior. Have you ever been on the receiving end of someone attacking you with criticisms? Do you remember how it felt? A client said: "The last time I was in a situation in which a person I deeply love criticized me, I felt as if I were being psychologically stabbed; it didn't make sense to me that because of a mistake I made, my whole person was being attacked."

SOFT LIKE A FEATHER: PLACATING

> *Matt: I told you, we have to go to dinner with my brother.*
> *Patricia: Matt, I would love to go but I have to prepare for a presentation for tomorrow and I'm behind.*
> *Matt: My brother likes to have everyone there and when we're back you can work on your presentation.*
> *Patricia: Matt, it will take me at least until 4 a.m. to be done and I'm presenting at 8 a.m. tomorrow.*
> *Matt: Aughh . . . I'm telling you again, my brother wants us to all be there and you're dating me, aren't you?*
> *Patricia: Fine, I'll just stay up all night working.*

Patricia felt conflicted and guilty, and didn't know what to do; in that moment, the only way she knew to handle conflict was going into feather mode by placating, putting her needs and desires under the rug. Solving a conflict was about the other person's needs, not about her needs or how to compromise in regard to a given situation.

COLD LIKE AN ICE CUBE: DISCONNECTING

When Ais and Dean were discussing their differences about how much time they spend with their in-laws, their conversation went like this:

> *Ais: I don't know if I can spend time with your mom today. I have tons of papers to write for grad school. I also get bored with her gossipy comments about the neighbors or how much money she used to make. It's quite obnoxious.*
> *Dean: Ais, feel free to keep talking; you can go on and on, as usual.*
> *Ais: I hate when you respond to me like this.*
>
> *Dean didn't respond to Ais's comments. He stood up, left the living room, and went to play a video game.*
>
> *Ais: Hello? Hello? Of course, now you just disconnect as if marriage is about that. Things get rocky and you simply check out; that's ridiculous.*
>
> *Dean physically removed himself from the situation, stopped talking to her, and went to sleep in the living room for the next five nights.*

Dean had had a long day at work and, after having that exchange with Ais, he felt hopeless and discouraged; the only way he knew to avoid feeling more overwhelmed was by disconnecting. That's what ice-cube behaviors look like when arguing.

Going into ice-cube mode is an emotional and physical disconnection; you're there, and you hear the other person, but you have shut down emotionally and nothing breaks your emotional walls. Like an ice cube, you come across as a cold person in those moments. What's the outcome of these ice-cube behaviors? Does it really help Dean's marriage to stonewall Ais?

Ice-cube behaviors when fighting can be easily confused with a time-out. A time-out is an agreement that you and whoever you're involved with have about taking a pause when the argument is going south and you both agree to return to it later. Ice-cube behaviors are an abrupt disconnection from the person you're struggling with.

If you rely on ice-cube behaviors when handling conflict, here is something for you to think about: you're hurting and the person in front of you is hurting too. When your emotional switch gets turned on to a maximum level so abruptly, you naturally want it to stop, but every time ice-cube mode dictates your behavior in a conflict and you remove yourself, you're removing yourself not only from the conflict but also from the relationship. Is that what you really want?

EXACT LIKE A CALCULATOR: MEASURING

> 66 Kyle and Joe are sitting at the dinner table, looking at each other. Kyle says, "Joe, I asked you to please be thoughtful when sharing our problems with others because I feel uncomfortable with my private life being exposed to people I don't even know, like your coworkers, the people you play basketball with, and your buddies from the gym." Joe looks at him and quickly says with a calm tone of voice, "You do the same thing

when talking to Mary, Lilly, and your other friends about us. If you talk to others about our private life, I can do it, too."

Going into measuring mode as your go-to conflict tactic when feeling upset is measuring and sizing up your partner's behaviors, as if you're playing tit-for-tat.

Exercise: Discerning the Purpose of Your Go-to Conflict Tactics

Bring to mind a fight you had recently and hold on to this image for a couple of moments in your mind. Zoom in a little bit more, noticing the moment in which the person you were arguing with said or did something upsetting to you. Can you recall that moment? If you take it a little bit further, can you recall what happened when you started getting upset? What was that upsetting emotion showing up for you? Was it frustration? Sadness? If your mind quickly says "anger," see if you can dig in a little bit and check whether the anger was masking any other sensation. When people upset us, we naturally have an emotional or a visceral reaction that shows up in our body. Can you tap into that? Can you notice the different thoughts that there were going on in your mind, one after another? Your mind may have had different types of thoughts about yourself, the person you were arguing with, even past experiences, and then quickly there is the urge to use your go-to conflict tactic. What happened under your skin after relying on your go-to tactic when handling this

argument? What did you feel?

Grab a piece of paper and write down the situation, all the thoughts, emotions, and sensations your emotional machinery came up with. Write down your go-to conflict tactic and what happened afterward.

It's hard to go into combat mode with others and, no doubt, we all do the best we can to handle them as they come. As a super-feeler, it's extra hard because your emotional switch goes on and amplifies these feelings to a maximum level at times: when you get hurt, you get *really* hurt; when you feel disappointed, you feel *really* disappointed; when you get angry, you get *really* angry. In those moments, you rely on what you have learned over the years: your go-to tactics to handle a fight.

If you pay attention, your go-to conflict tactics are quick responses to manage your hurt and all those feelings that come when you're arguing. Who wouldn't use them when hurting? Using any of these conflict tactics here and there is one thing, but overusing them is a different story. Your conflict tactics may have become quick fixes and overlearned behaviors for those uncomfortable emotions.

Core Skill: Noticing Your Conflict Tactics

For this exercise choose a particular type of relationship to work with. Grab a piece of paper and draw a vertical line down the middle of the page. On the left side, write the different conflicts you have had in that type of relationship, and on the right side, write down how you solved the struggle or which conflict tactics you used.

Completing this exercise may be a bit tricky because people may have done very upsetting things to you, and you may even still feel upset, but looking at how you handled conflict is a step toward taming your emotional machinery so you can have the relationships you want to have.

After you complete your list, ask yourself: Do my go-to conflict tactics work in my relationships? Within ACT, we always go back to examining the workability of a behavior. To examine this more deeply, take a look at the inventory of your go-to tactics, choose a particular example, and then answer the next questions:

1. What happens in the moment of the fight?
    Cues: what happens to your sensations, urges, thoughts, and emotions when using your go-to conflict tactics? Do they go away? Do they stay? Do they get better or worse?
2. What's the long-term outcome for your relationship?
3. What's the long-term outcome for yourself?

Does it work to constantly blame, make threats, disconnect, attack a person, explain hundreds of times why you do what you do, or measure your partner's behavior? I'm willing to bet that your go-to conflict tactics work in the moment in that you may get what you want; however, in the long term, if you have been overusing them, it's quite likely that your relationship won't survive and you end up with more frustration, sadness, and disconnection.

Is It Time to Make a Shift?

Fighting with others is hard, and yet it can be a moment of strengthening for a relationship — or the beginning of a broken one. Having disagreements, disputes, and differences of opinion with the people we love is necessary in order to have real relationships, instead of fake ones. Learning to have a fair fight is a core competence, and the next chapters will show you how to fight in a way that is consistent with how you want to be in a relationship. Having a fair fight doesn't mean that you'll get everything you want, but it means that at the end of it, you will know you did your best to live your interpersonal values. Arguing is hard for everyone involved in the argument: it's hard for you and it's hard for others; however, when your emotional switch is on, it's difficult to look at the other person and be . . .

Chapter 29: In Your Shoes: Curious and Empathic Behaviors

> " While walking in the park, Tim holds Johanna's hand and says, "I'm having one of those moments when I see you texting on the phone and I wonder whether I can trust that you are telling me the truth right now."
>
> Johanna looks at him and says, "Get used to it; I text all the time. Welcome to my world of distrust. Now you know how it feels: before you used to ask me about my best friend, now it's about whether I'm texting another guy. You don't hear me, you are manipulating the conversation, it's smothering and controlling, and no, you cannot change me." Tim looks at her and, after taking a deep breath, doesn't say anything.

Which go-to conflict tactic did Johanna rely on? Tim was still confused about how, after saying, "I'm triggered and having one of those moments," the conversation unfolded into comments about him being controlling, smothering, and asking her to change. Johanna, on her side, was deeply hurt because she felt she was reconnecting with Tim, as she hadn't felt in a while, and while listening to his comments, her inner voice came up with the thoughts "Nothing is working, nothing is getting better." She felt frustrated and hopeless about their relationship. She then quickly went into calculator and wheel mode as her go-to tactics and couldn't see Tim's fears and discomfort. Johanna was too focused on her own experience, as if Tim's emotional experience didn't exist. Have you been there?

When you get hurt, your emotional switch turns on, and you are in the middle of a battle, it's hard to see what the other person is going through because you're hurting and consumed by your own experience. It's understandable, and yet the question is: is it effective for your relationship?

It's hard to learn from others' struggles when you're hurting, but it's one of the most valuable skills for having a fair fight: to really understand what the other person is thinking, feeling, or sensing when they are hurting. How do you do it?

Curious Behaviors: From Your Hurt to the Other Person's Hurt

You don't have to like, love, or agree with what others say when you're having a fight; you still can learn about it, even when your emotional switch is on. Curiosity in your relationships is about learning from the other person, especially when they're hurting.

What are the advantages of practicing curious behaviors when fighting? Your relationship grows because the people involved in it are speaking about their struggles, hurts, and disappointments, instead of sweeping them under the rug. When people hide their struggles from each other, and then go into rugging mode, there is less of a chance to have fulfilling, long-lasting, and real relationships.

Core Skill: Practicing Curious Behaviors

The next time you're in an argument follow these steps:

1. Notice and name your emotions.
2. Notice any urges or thoughts you have to start your go-to conflict tactics.
3. Practice defusion: instead of acting based on them so quickly, name them (e.g., little angry cartoons, sassy cartoons, and so on; you can even imagine they're little cartoons starring the other person).
4. Ground yourself with your breathing, press your feet really hard into the ground, and do your best to get out of your mind.
5. Focus on the other person by asking a single question about their hurt.

I get it, it's hard, and yet, it's one of most important skills to creating a long-lasting relationship. When I invite my clients to practice this skill, they usually go into reason-giving mode, listing 101 reasons why it is still hard, or they giggle, and in their giggling, there is fear in their eyes. Is your inner voice doing that? Are you getting hooked on those thoughts? I know it's challenging to get out of your own hurt and tune in to the other person's hurt in the middle of a battle. But practicing curious behaviors while battling is doable and is taking a step toward creating the relationship you want to have. Practice and patience will take you further.

If you're willing to shift your attention from inward to outward, with curiosity, instead of getting hooked on inner judgments and relying on your go-to fighting tactics, what comes next?

Empathic Behaviors

Being kind and understanding with others is one behavior, but being kind and understanding when you are arguing is a different behavior. Daniel Goleman (1995) speaks about the core elements of empathic behaviors: learn what people think about something, learn about the feelings they have about it, and check in with them about what you can do about it.

Core Skill: Practicing Empathic Behaviors

To practice being empathic, ask the person you are having a conflict with the following questions: "What is concerning about the particular challenging situation you are upset about?" "What are you feeling about it?" and "What might help solve the situation?" If you ask them at least three questions, you will be surprised to see how it makes a shift in your relationship in the long term. It works because people see that you get them!

Let Go of Having the Last Word

Practicing curious and empathic behaviors is the beginning of a shift, and yet, you may still struggle with letting go of the argument. How often do you get hooked on thoughts like "I need to make a point," "I wish you didn't say that," or "I only said that because," and then the back and forth begins all over again. Ask yourself, "What is the outcome of getting hooked on these thoughts about my relationship?" and "Is it really workable to get the last word in when arguing?" If it isn't, are you open to letting go of having the last word?

Creating the relationships you want to have requires a lot of dancing with all of your emotions; sometimes you stand on their feet, and sometimes they trip you up, especially when you're fighting. And yet, a well-lived life is one with strong connections with others even though there may also be conflict. Part of maintaining those strong connections is being able to effectively give and receive feedback so each other's needs are being met. Sound challenging? Read on.

Chapter 30: Giving and Receiving Feedback

> ❝❝ *I love the Virgin brand, I really do. Which is why I continue to use it despite a series of unfortunate incidents over the last few years. This latest incident takes the biscuit. You don't get to a position like yours, Richard, with anything less than a generous sprinkling of observational power, so I know you will have spotted the tomato next to the two yellow shafts of sponge [cake] on the left. Yes, it's next to the sponge [cake] shaft without the green paste [icing]. That's got to be the clue, hasn't it? No sane person would serve a dessert with a tomato, would they?"*

In 2008, Sir Richard Branson, a renowned entrepreneur and founder of Virgin airlines, received a letter from a passenger who took a flight from Mumbai (India) to Heathrow (London); the sentences above are from the letter. This letter went viral because of the format in which it was written: it was a real complaint letter, and yet, it was funny.

Giving and receiving feedback are core skills when dealing with others, and they will help you not only foster long-lasting relationships with the people you care about but also handle all types of conflicts in your life. Let's begin.

Core Skill: Making Specific Requests (aka Giving Feedback)

As long as we're alive we all have moments in which we ask the people around us to stop, start, or do more or less of something; it's a very natural and understandable part of any relationship, and it actually helps the relationship grow. Here are the basic components of making an effective request: Be specific about what you're asking. Clearly state 1) what the situation is, 2) your thoughts about it, 3) your emotions when dealing with it, and 4) your request.

Below are two examples of requests. Choose the one that is most effective.

- I would like you to be healthy and take care of your body.
- On Monday evening when we were talking about the outing with your friends, I reflected that the last four times you went out, you came home drunk and after midnight. I've actually been thinking about your health and safety, and I get stressed and worried that something may happen to you. So, I want to ask you to please stop drinking as much as you have been doing the last five nights.

Asking effectively for what you need is a very useful skill to have, and it really helps you be the person you want to be instead of going into shark behaviors when requesting something from others. You may not get everything you ask for, but it's a starting point for having a healthy relationship.

Core Skill: Differentiating Feedback from Character Attacks

Sooner or later people around you are going to make a comment about the piece of furniture you bought, how your hair looks, the type of work you do, and all types of things about you and around you; sometimes they will give you explicit and direct feedback, and other times they will simply make comments about stuff around you. As a super-feeler, here are the challenges you're facing:

1. To learn to separate comments people make about you as a person versus comments they make about your behavior (e.g., perceiving the comment "you seem to be looking around all over today when watching the movie" as something is wrong with you).

2. To learn to receive direct criticisms, opinions, and feedback that others may have about you and your behaviors at some point.

> ❝❝ Samantha, a contractor working for a mental health facility, received an e-mail from her supervisor asking her to complete her charts before Friday and let her know when they're done so she can proceed with her monthly payment. Samantha read this e-mail and felt a wave of heat rise in her face. She felt she had been accused of shirking her responsibilities, and her inner voice quickly came up with thoughts along the lines of, "She thinks I'm lazy and I don't do my job well."
>
> Samantha got hooked on those feelings and thoughts, and she hastily sent an e-mail to her supervisor: "I'm not lazy or irresponsible. I don't like how you think of me and treat me; it's illegal to retain my salary, and you should be thoughtful when reviewing my charts, because you always disorganize them."
>
> In the heat of the moment, Samantha forgot that she was actually

a contractor, was e-mailing her supervisor, and that her contract specified that in order to get paid she needed to accomplish specific tasks, such as completing her charts.

The following week, Samantha was let go from her job because her supervisor stated that in less than five months, she had received more than six e-mails from Samantha that came across as disrespectful and impulsive; her supervisor stated that she had tried to talk to Samantha about them every time, but unfortunately, nothing seemed to work.

Have you been in Samantha's shoes? She felt what she felt, whether right or wrong, justified or not. Samantha's emotional switch turned on and she got hooked on it and the thoughts that her inner voice came up with; she didn't have the skill to step back from the situation, stay with her feelings without acting based on them, check her values, and then choose her behavior. Samantha got angry, didn't check her own angry reaction, and didn't know how to separate her supervisor's feedback about completing tasks from feeling blamed as a person.

Look within, especially when you are feeling angry, attacked, accused, or unseen, to name a few emotions you learned about in the section above, and ask yourself these key questions:

1. What is the emotion? Can you name the emotion?
2. How does it feel in your body?
3. What does your inner voice tell you about it? Is your inner voice telling you anything about you in particular?
4. What are the impulses or go-to actions that come with it?
5. If you pause and step back from the situation, is that emotion

familiar? Is your inner voice getting hooked on the narrative about how people wronged you or hurt you? If you peel back the anger, what's the underlying emotion that really hurts? Is your emotional trilogy of abandonment, rejection, and loneliness activated? Or are feelings from isolation city, like shame and guilt, showing up for you?

6. Check in with your values.

7. Choose your behavior about the situation: curious and empathic behaviors are very handy as new behaviors to try.

Receiving feedback is a core skill and your emotional machinery can make it really hard when it's on, but the more you practice the skills you're learning in these chapters, the better it's going to be. Remember to practice the curious and empathic behaviors you learned in the previous chapter in order to give and receive feedback effectively. This will help you manage conflict in a way that moves you closer to your values and the relationships you want to have.

Chapter 31: Tying It All Together

You just finished learning about very important skills that will improve your relationships right away, if you put them into practice. Let's do a brief wrap-up: you identified your interpersonal values (chapter 25), examined your relatedness style (chapter 26), and then explored methods of your nonverbal communication (chapter 27).

And because relationships get messy, you learned about your go-to conflict tactics when you feel hurt, such as blaming, demanding, giving reasons, attacking someone's character, placating, disconnecting, and measuring (chapter 28). You learned how to have a fair fight by practicing curious and empathic behaviors when dealing with conflict without damaging your relationship (chapter 29), and how to effectively give and accept feedback (chapter 30).

Here is an example of how Maggie, who we met in earlier "Tying It All Together" chapters, used all these skills when dealing with a conflict at work:

> *During a meeting with her supervisor, Maggie, a super-feeler, was asked why her reports weren't completed before Friday, even though she had received an e-mail about it. Maggie noticed a wave of heat in her body, felt blamed and felt*

wrongly accused, and heard her inner voice shout thoughts at her like, "I'm tired of playing these games! Who does she think she is?" In the next moment, when looking at her supervisor's face, Maggie had a strong urge to go into knife mode and tell her how obnoxious she was when giving feedback and how disorganized she was with her own work; she also had an urge to go into hammer mode and demand she put her charts in alphabetical order before handing them back to Maggie.

Maggie realized she wasn't at her best; she intentionally slowed her breathing down and checked in with herself about what really mattered to her with regard to this conflict. She noticed that in the relationship with her supervisor and at work in general, she strives to be cooperative. Then she apologized for not having it done, requested an extension, asked her supervisor about her expectations about the task, the rationale behind having it done by the 20th of every month, instead of the 30th, and then sought her supervisor's advice so that next month she wouldn't struggle with the task.

Maggie left the meeting with a strong sense of relief about handling it differently than her emotions were pushing her to do.

SECTION VI

Me in This Moment

Chapter 32: It's All About Mindfulness

We're living in a time of a mindfulness revolution: mindfulness here, mindfulness there, and mindfulness everywhere. The word *mindfulness* has become a popular word in mainstream culture; it's in scientific writings, self-help books, and TV news. Newspapers announce when politicians, Hollywood actors, or sports players practice it, and even YouTube has all types of mindfulness videos, from the most serious to the silliest, and everything in between. Something must be going on with mindfulness, right? The answer is yes.

The research on mindfulness has been exploding the last twenty years, and its outcomes are unquestionable. I won't review the research on it because it's beyond the scope of this book, and I don't want you to get bored with my geeky side. But I do have a comment for the super-feelers reading this book: applying mindfulness to your life has benefits, period.

Are you fully present right now when reading this book? Check for yourself. Are you distracted with the background noise in your mind and random thoughts showing up? Are you paying attention to sounds from the street? Do you notice how you feel in your current body posture? Are you focused on each word when reading this book? Being present with the outside and the inside world is not easy, especially if your emotional switch is on. And yet, you can learn to intentionally be here, right now, and reap the benefits of living with awareness.

Mindfulness is paying attention or being aware with intention of what's happening in this moment under your skin and in your surroundings for what it is, not as your feelings tell you it is. (Throughout this section, we'll interchangeably use *mindfulness* and *awareness*.)

Misconceptions About Mindfulness

Before moving forward, let's go over a couple of misconceptions about mindfulness.

POKER FACE OR PUPPY FACE WHEN PRACTICING MINDFULNESS?

Being mindful doesn't mean that you have to have a serious look by tensing your facial muscles, looking down, and making sure you don't smile or even blink because you fear that you're not being mindful.

On the other hand, practicing mindfulness is not about looking like the Dalai Lama. A former client started a session by saying to me, "Dr. Z., it's not me, I don't have it within me to be mindful. I don't have the sweet and peaceful face that the Dalai Lama has when he meditates. It's just not me." Have you had a thought along those lines or similar ones? You may or may not have a puppy face when you are being mindful, but learning to be mindful is not about forcing yourself to make sure you look peaceful, calm, or serene.

Practicing mindfulness is not only a very individualized activity, it's also an activity that by its very nature shifts from moment to moment because every moment we're alive is different. No moment is the same as the one before. Sometimes you may have a peaceful look, other times a poker face, and you may have many other types of faces as well; there are no rules about having a "mindful" face.

IS MINDFULNESS AN EMOTIONAL VACUUM?

Here are two very popular misconceptions of mindfulness: "I was so upset, and then I used mindfulness, and everything was fine," or "I was so upset, I did mindfulness, and it didn't work." Which one do you relate to more? Incorporating mindfulness practices into your daily life is both an intentional way of being and a skill of paying attention in the moment to whatever shows up without trying to change anything. It means letting your emotions, sensations, thoughts, images, and memories simply be, even if those feelings are anxiety, sadness, or distress.

DOES MINDFULNESS WORK ONLY WHEN YOU ARE RELAXED?

In a world that moves so fast that reality changes in the blink of an eye, it's natural you would want to be hassle-free, stress-free, and as calm as possible. It's understandable that anything that may look like it could give us a sense of peace is appealing and attractive to us. Let me break the news to you: mindfulness is not about being relaxed or mellow-yellow. That's not the purpose of it, and if that is your goal, it will defeat mindfulness's core function: to pay attention to the moment as it is. Are you relaxed at all times? Quite likely not; I'm certainly not. We are all wired to experience all types of feelings, sensations, and urges, and being relaxed is just one emotional state.

CAN YOU MINDFULLY MURDER?

In the middle of a conversation about the mindfulness revolution, and the ups and downs of it, a friend asked, "Can you kill someone mindfully?" Here is my response: If mindfulness is about paying attention with intention and purpose, then yes, you can mindfully murder someone.

But would you really like your life to be about murdering with intent? Is mindfulness only about attention training, or is it more related to consciously pausing and learning to pay attention to why we do what we do? Mindfulness, in my humble opinion, is more the latter.

Mindfulness is a practice, not necessarily one that is quick and dirty, but one that is rich and deep and as simple as it looks.

ARE MINDFULNESS AND MEDITATION THE SAME THING?

We could spend hundreds of pages discussing and reviewing this, but here is a short response: mindfulness is an umbrella and meditation is a type of mindfulness under it.

Why Awareness for Super-Feelers?

As a super-feeler, you're biological wired to have intense feelings, and because of this and your temperament and learning history, it's easy to get caught up in those strong emotions, sensations, and urges, doing everything you can to manage them, without checking whether your response is effective or not, helpful or not, adaptive or not, in a given moment. It's as if you have an emotional switch that turns on and off.

Your sensitivity to feelings makes you unique in many ways because you're finely attuned to a broad range of emotions in a way that others are not. And naturally, you can see others' struggles, suffering, and difficulties as if you have a magnifying lens on their emotional world. It's when you're hurting with overwhelming emotions, crushed with distressful feelings, or defeated with overpowering impulses that life is hard for you and the people around you.

It's a living hell when your emotions are dragging you like a puppet all over the place, up and down, left and right. Learning to observe when you're being stomped on by these beastie emotions, coming back to your feet to tame them, and choosing your behavior will help you move toward what matters to you: your values. Now it's time to learn awareness skills so that you can learn to dance with your emotions, without them stepping on your life.

Chapter 33: Mindfulness in Action

Let's stop talking about mindfulness and do mindfulness. Below you will find a brief menu of mindfulness exercises from the low-key ones to the more complex ones. See what works for you, and remember, mindfulness is not necessarily about stopping your hurt, becoming relaxed, or feeling positive.

Have you noticed how food delivery company services are growing and growing? You can have gourmet dishes from fancy restaurants to homemade meals that taste like they were made in your grandma's kitchen. Because we live in a world in which things can be had on the go, there is no reason why mindfulness cannot be practiced on the go. You don't need to squeeze extra time into your already busy schedule. You can start right now, right here.

Exercise: Mindfulness on the Go

When performing the next exercises, simply describe to yourself what you hear, sense, touch, taste, and see. Describing doesn't involve judgments of good or bad, right or wrong; describing is simple saying to yourself what your senses notice.

❑ When walking, notice the weight of your body on your legs, your feet, the movement of your arms, and the pace of your steps; are you walking slowly or briskly? Notice the coordination between your legs, arms, and back, and your overall posture.

❑ When talking, observe the openness of your mouth, the position of your tongue when pronouncing different sounds, any tension on your lips, the pace of your speech, and the rhythm of your communication.

❑ When holding your cell phone, see if you can pause, take a single deep breath, and then notice the pressure of your fingers when holding the phone. Notice whether you are using all your fingers or some of them. Is one finger having more pressure than others? Do you place the phone touching your ear or close to your ear?

Now that you have the basics of how you can practice being present in the moment within your daily routine, see if you can come up with other daily activities to practice mindfulness. If you practice this skill once a day, that's a beginning, and little by little you will reap the benefits of it.

Mindfulness in the Room

Let's turn your mindfulness practice up a notch, and for these exercises you're going to require a minimum of 5 minutes to a maximum of 10 minutes in your day. Up for it? I'm not asking you to block off a half hour of your day, or a whole weekend for a silent retreat; I'm inviting you to make a choice about dedicating 5 to 10 minutes of your busy schedule to learn to step back and get a grip on your overwhelming emotions. Remember, what we practice, grows.

Exercise: Mindful Observation

It's helpful if you have a timer for this exercise. Read the directions first so you know what to expect and can pace yourself with it.

Choose any object for this exercise. Begin by sitting in a comfortable position and focusing your eyes on that object. Place the object in front of you.

Take a few slow, deep breaths, and gently do your best to breathe in through your nose, and out through your mouth. Then, without touching the object, begin looking at it and exploring its different surfaces with your eyes. What does the surface of the object look like? What shape does it have? Does it have multiple sides? Is it shiny or dull? What color is it? Does it have multiple colors or a single color? Take your time exploring what the object looks like.

Next, hold the object and notice its weight in your hands. You can even move your arms with it to capture its heaviness or lightness. Does it feel smooth or rough? Hot or cold in your fingers? Is it bendable or rigid? Bring it a bit closer to your nose and notice any particular smell it has. Keep exploring this object for a couple more minutes.

Because your mind is active 24/7, it's natural that some thoughts will show up while completing this exercise. Notice the thoughts, memories, images, or any other associations that arrive, and return back to the object. Is there anything unique about this object? After a couple of moments, place the object out of your sight, and go back to noticing your breathing.

Exercise: Mindful Posture

For this exercise, you can be sitting, standing, or lying down. Choose a position that feels comfortable.

To start, see if you prefer to close your eyes or keep them open, and gently pay attention to your breathing, noticing each time you breathe in and breathe out; slow your pace so you can help your body slow down. Next, notice the alignment of your back; is it straight or bent? Notice the alignment between your neck and head. Are you hunching, leaning forward, or leaning backward? See if you can adjust the alignment between your back, neck, and head into a single line that is not rigid like a stick but straight in a comfortable upright, natural way; let your chin naturally find its posture by resting along with your head. Whether you're sitting down, standing up, or lying down, let your arms naturally and effortlessly hang, with your hands resting as well.

Now notice any tension point in your body as you scan from the top to the bottom and from the bottom to the top. You can start by scanning for any tightness, stiffness, or tension in your face, starting with your forehead, eyes, cheeks, and jaw, and then slowly move to your neck, shoulders, chest, torso, hips, legs, back, and feet.

Lastly, see if you can find the center of balance in your body. If you're standing or sitting down, rock your body gently and slowly from the left to the right, and forward and backward, until it naturally finds the middle posture, the center; once you find it, stay there for a couple of moments, practicing stillness.

The list of private mindfulness exercises that require you to schedule time apart is inexhaustible; check eastbaybehaviortherapycenter.com for a list of the ones I use.

Mindfulness Like a Pro

We're moving on to another level of mindfulness. Let me say a few words before we start: You're not obligated to practice mindfulness, but doing it, in one form or another, by noticing your chores or daily activities, taking the time to pause, sit, and notice your surroundings and what's happening under your skin, will make a difference in your life as a super-feeler. No one is better than you at checking how you're approaching mindfulness up to this point.

Exercise: Dropping the Rope

For the next exercise, find a quiet place, and schedule 15 to 20 minutes of your time; it's helpful if you have a device to record yourself reading the directions with a soft and slow tone of voice, then listen to your recording and follow the directions.

Get in a comfortable position, standing or sitting down. Close your eyes or focus your gaze on a single point, then take a few slow, deep breaths. Take at least one minute to get centered in this position.

For the next moments get in touch with an emotion that you usually run away from and avoid at all costs, and let's call this your target for this exercise. While focusing on this emotion, do your best to stay in touch with that feeling and watch how your body responds. Do you notice any bodily sensations arising? Scan your body from the top to the bottom. While focusing on your body, your mind may come up with all types of emotional noise like ghost thoughts, fantasies, forecasting, narrating, or ruling thoughts. See if you can notice them without getting trapped by them, and shift your attention back to your target emotion and its particular bodily sensation.

Notice where the sensation begins and ends; notice exactly where it is in your body. If you could make a sculpture in the shape of this sensation, what would it look like? Observe whether this sensation is pushing you to stay with it or to suppress it, push it down, and distract yourself. After noticing the impulses that come with this sensation, see if you can completely "drop the rope" and stop the fight by simply noticing, describing, and observing this sensation without doing anything about it. What about if instead of fighting against it you chose to have it, exactly as it is? If you are still resisting, do your best again to just drop the rope, drop the fight.

Do your best to notice this feeling, along with its sensations, noticing what comes instead of running away from it. See what happens if you choose to feel this particular emotion. You don't have to like it or dislike it; you're just invited to feel it as it is, without fighting against it.

Is there anything truly dangerous, harmful, or hostile about this emotion that still pushes you to get rid of it? Can you experience this emotion as it comes, as it is? See if you can drop the rope from this unpleasant feeling just a little bit more; see if you can actually get to this emotion by choice, instead of running away from it. See if right now you can stay with this one emotion.

Next, see if you can get in contact with the person behind your eyes, the observer you that is watching this emotion and is watching your body having these feelings, sensations, thoughts, memories, and images. What do you notice?

Now, from the place of looking at that emotion and feeling and having it, can you sense an urge or a pull toward action? What do you want to do when you feel this? Instead of just doing that behavior or trying to suppress it, stay exactly where you are and feel what it feels like to notice the pull to take action, without actually taking action. Now ask yourself, "Is there anything in this pull that I cannot have or is fundamentally bad or dangerous that could destroy me?"

Notice your breathing and take a few good, deep breaths with the air coming in through your nose and out of your mouth. Ask yourself: "Am I willing to go on from here carrying all these reactions wherever I go, noticing how they come and then simply having them?" Gently open your eyes and bring yourself back to the room.

Any reactions to this exercise? You're feeling, having a feeling, learning to feel that emotion, and noticing the pull between taking action and not taking action.

Chapter 34: Tying It All Together

You made it! You just gained another important skill in your course on emotion strategy designed especially for super-feelers. You learned about the benefits of mindfulness and why it is an important skill for you, we clarified any misconceptions about it (chapter 32) and then, you practiced a variety of awareness exercises, with different durations and focal points (chapter 33).

Me, My New Map, and the World We Live In

Chapter 35: Life Has Messy Moments

While I was writing this book, a friend of mine lost her home and all her belongings in the wildfires in Santa Rosa, California; Hurricane Irma destroyed part of Puerto Rico; and I was robbed at a coffee shop, losing a 24/7 tool: my laptop, and with it, the book you're now reading.

If we look back at our lives and our friends' lives, we'll recognize a collection of misfortunate situations, such as misplacing our favorite high heels, losing our darling pet, failing a class, feeling rejected by a person we love, struggling financially, and on and on. Life has many messy moments.

We don't know when natural disasters are coming, or when accidents will happen, or whether people will hurt us or not. I certainly didn't know that on Sunday morning, twelve days before my deadline to turn in this book, I would be robbed at a coffee shop by young adults.

When unexpected and painful things happen, our emotional switch turns on, and there is a turmoil of emotions we go through; they throw us up and down, left and right. We don't dance with emotions with rhythm and grace; instead, we stomp on anger, stumble with sadness, trip on rage, or fall down on sorrow. It's hard.

I can honestly tell you that after I was robbed I lived an emotional hell for three days; my emotional switch was on and off and it dragged me around like a puppet. It wasn't easy; I didn't feel like myself and my body was on edge constantly. And yet, over and over, I used all the skills you learned in this book.

I noticed how quickly my emotions of frustration, disappointment, hurt, and sadness got activated throughout the day; I named them as "the robbery feelings," acknowledged them in my body, recognized their strong urge to act based on anger, and took a deep breath, over and over, just to be able to step back and check what was really important in that moment, such as paying attention to cooking dinner, listening to the person in front of me, measuring the height to hang a painting on the wall, and so on. I went through that cycle hundreds of times; it wasn't easy to practice these skills, and yet they were very handy.

I was careful not to engage in hours of dwelling about the robbery because it was so easy to slip into the waterfall of angry thoughts and get stuck in cranky town. I shared with friends and family what I could, when I could, and carefully noticed when my body was getting too agitated. Then I breathed and paused. It wasn't easy to get unstuck, call the publisher, squirming with embarrassment, and request an extension.

It was on the fourth or fifth day of being in emotional misery that my body slowly went back to its natural baseline; I didn't have nightmares about the robbery, I wasn't organizing my actions around anger, and I wasn't the puppet of my emotions any longer. I was still upset, sad, and disappointed, but instead of fighting against those emotions, minimizing them, or pretending they weren't there, I knew that the best thing I could do was to let them be. I made space for them, even though I didn't like them at all.

Life gets messy, and yet, using all the ACT skills in this book helped me get through a tough moment. We really don't have control over how life goes, even though we wish we did.

The Illusion of Control

There are things you can change and you have control over, and there are things you don't. For example, if it's too cold, I can turn on the heater; if it's too dark, I can turn on the lights. There are problems that can be solved, controlled, and repaired by your direct actions; do you recognize some of those problems that can be solved in your life right now?

There are things that simply are what they are; we don't like them, we may even hate them, and yet, that's how they are. For example, I cannot change what happened that Sunday morning, I cannot change the cold weather right now, and I cannot change that we live in an unfair world. I'm not saying you shouldn't advocate to change unfair situations; I'm just saying that when your emotional machinery turns on, you need to distinguish between what you can change and what you cannot change, and choose your behavior according to your values, not according to a change agenda or control agenda.

In this moment, if you step back, do you find yourself trying to change a situation? If so, what's the outcome? Is behaving on the change agenda taking you closer or further away from your values? Are you still hooked on a wishful thought?

WISHFUL THOUGHT: I WISH THEY WOULD CHANGE

Have people badly disappointed you? Did your friends break your trust? Were you excluded from gatherings with others? Have you been cheated on?

Learning to live, create the relationships you want to have, and become the person you want to be comes with all types of struggles, including people doing things, saying things, and behaving in ways that simply hurt you. Whether it's intentional or not, people hurt you. Sometimes you see it coming like a meteorologist sees the weather conditions for the day; other times, people catch you by surprise with their behaviors, as happens in scary movies. It's hard, and I get it, because I've been there, too.

Let me break some news to you: a device to control people's behaviors has not been invented yet and is not being sold on Amazon.

You don't have power over how others behave, think, feel, sense, or whatever else is related to their behavior. Quite likely you already know that, as many of my clients do, and yet when there is a struggle, their inner voice quickly comes up with thoughts like "I wish they would change; I just hoped they wouldn't do that; why can't they just do things differently?" and the list goes on and on. Has your inner voice come up with thoughts like that? As you know by now, your inner voice is doing its job, and it comes with all types of creations: ruling, forecasting, retelling, labeling, and narrating thoughts too.

Wishful thoughts are fun to have at times because they can take you into fantasy land, like when I find myself wishing I would win the lottery and I see myself jumping from plane to plane visiting London, drinking Scotch in Scotland, and so on, and the next thing I know, I am in my own la-la land in my head; three hours have passed and I haven't written anything, and then I feel bad because of my agreement and commitment to the publisher.

Other times wishful thoughts can be little hooks into more anger, disappointment, and a change agenda, like when Charlie, a super-feeler, gets into an argument with his sister. He gets so frustrated with how she manages her career life that his inner voice goes on and on about how he wishes she would do things differently, listen to him, and do more of what he says. Next, Charlie ends up calling her, repeating himself over and over, getting a headache talking to her, and noticing how, while his sister goes into cranky town, he goes into regretting land.

Wishful thoughts are tricky, and as you're familiar with by now, workability is the yardstick. My biggest advice to you is to study whether wishful thoughts about "others changing" are workable or not in your life.

Your Past Is Your Past

Have awful things happened to you that you wish hadn't happened to you or anyone you care about? Have you been exposed to trauma such as abuse, natural disasters, or life accidents? Or maybe you grew up in a family in which everything looked fine on paper, with married parents and successful careers, and yet you were hurting. What's the story that you carry from your past?

I don't know you, and I don't know your history or your hurts, but I know that if you're reading this book it's because you went through a lot and still care about what's important to you.

Here is another piece of tough news I have for you: your past is your past, and there is nothing you can do to change it.

I'm not saying that what you went through is right or should be forgotten, because that wouldn't be fair. But in this moment, I would like to invite you to step back and study the workability of fusing with thoughts like "This shouldn't ever have happened to me," "I'm emotional because of what I went through," or "I've become a fearful person because of what my parents did to me." I know it's already painful to have those thoughts, they are hard to sit with, and yet, letting them run your behaviors is hurting you more.

When your emotional machinery keeps you trapped in those thoughts about the past, what do you do? What steps do you take in the moment? And here is the fundamental ACT question: are those steps in the direction of your values?

If your answer is yes, kudos to you, and keep moving toward what matters. If your answer is no, consider the following question: which ACT skills and steps do you need to take toward your values? Remember, living your values is not about living an impeccable life but a life you choose. If you've reached your tipping point, read on.

Chapter 36: Your Tipping Point

Sometimes you're hurting so badly, as if you're living in emotional hell every day, that you cannot hide from it any longer, and you want to do something about it. You may or may not have reached that place, but if you're still reading this book it's because you are ready to stop the agony that hurts you. You're ready to make a shift in your life. This is your tipping point.

Malcolm Gladwell, in his book *The Tipping Point: How Little Things Can Make a Difference*, explains the process in which a change, any change, increases dramatically beyond a certain point. The tipping point, as a phrase, originates from physics and has been applied in many fields, from economics and human ecology to epidemiology and social psychology. In this book, we refer to the tipping point as the point at which a new behavior or a new skill starts a path of change for you.

At times, it's impossible to hide from our pain, it's bigger than us, and in those moments, we know that unless we make a change, nothing good will come to us.

Years ago, after running a training clinic for over seven years with tons of dedication and commitment, and after spending hundreds of hours putting it together, I knew that little by little it was time to let it go. Yet I was petrified at the idea of letting go of something I had started from scratch, and I postponed the idea every year; my mind usually went into reasoning mode and found a good excuse to stay and not let go.

Overall, I was feeling excited about meeting new doctoral students, supervising, teaching, and doing a little bit of clinical research, but I was also feeling resentful and cranky about not having more time to do other projects that were very important to me, like writing and developing intensive programs. It all came down to a moment when, while attending an ACT workshop, I was asked to focus on a particularly difficult and troublesome situation. I quickly noticed all the directions that my emotions were pulling me in; it was in that moment I learned that I could no longer hide from my fears and in tears had to acknowledge every single escape strategy I had been using: making excuses for myself, postponing the decision, telling myself, "What if I make a mistake; what if I don't make it; what if my mentor gets upset with me and refuses to work with me?" I felt extremely sad, disappointed, and scared, but I just couldn't stop hiding from my pain. That was my tipping point. That day, I resigned.

In less than eight months I submitted two book proposals, got both of them accepted, felt invigorated by new projects, and started a new intensive program for people with obsessive-compulsive disorders. I still have thoughts about making a mistake; I still have doubtful thoughts about my capacity, and I feel nostalgic at times about my old position. It wasn't easy, but I couldn't run away from my own hurt any longer. It was time to make a shift.

The life of a super-feeler is not an easy one; it takes courage to be in your shoes and not be dragged around by the emotional machinery all the time. Change is possible, and becoming the best version of yourself is possible too, no matter where you are in life right now.

The next section summarizes all the emotion strategy skills you have learned in this book, one by one, and it shows you your new map for moving forward.

Moving Forward: Your New Map

Throughout all these chapters you have studied in detail your emotional machinery and learned key skills in emotion strategy to manage those moments when your emotional switch gets started and pushes you in all directions.

The chart below summarizes all the skills you have been learning; they are organized as inner and outer skills. Inner skills are skills you do privately, and you are the only one aware of them; outer skills are behaviors that you do that are observable by others. Next to each skill you have the chapter number for reference so you can go back and revisit a specific skill.

Noticing and Naming Skills

Noticing and naming urges for quick fixes
Chapter 2

Noticing the function of your emotions
Chapter 6

Noticing and naming your emotions: fleeting, overwhelming, chronic emotions, and gut reactions
Chapters 8, 9, 11, 12

Noticing your emotional chains
Chapter 9

Noticing and naming body states: flight, fight, or freeze mode
Chapter 21

Noticing and naming go-to conflict tactics/modes: hammer, wheel, computer, knife, feather, computer, measuring, ice cube
Chapter 28

Defusion Skills

Defusing from beliefs about emotions
Chapter 5

Defusion from beliefs about anger
Chapter 10

Defusing from retelling, ruling, labeling, and forecasting thoughts
Chapters 16, 17

Defusing from narrating thoughts about yourself and others
Chapter 18

Defusing from conflictive thoughts about conflict
Chapter 28

Defusing from misconceptions about mindfulness
Chapter 32

Checking Skills

Checking your personal, health, and interpersonal values
Chapters 4, 19, 25

Checking the function of your emotions and thoughts
Chapters 6, 15

Checking the workability of your behaviors toward your values
Chapter 7

Checking the function of your go-to conflict tactics
Chapter 28

Acceptance Skills

Choosing to feel and accept
Chapter 13

Choosing to accept reality
Chapter 35

Awareness Skills

Awareness/mindfulness exercises
Chapter 33

Body-Based Skills

Grounding exercises
Chapters 10, 21

Stretching exercises
Chapter 23

Soothing exercises
Chapter 23

Interpersonal Skills

Choosing your body posture, face, and voice
Chapter 27

Empathic behaviors
Chapter 29

Making specific requests to others
Chapter 30

Receiving feedback from others
Chapter 30

Differentiating feedback from character attacks
Chapter 30

HOW TO USE THE CHART

How do you use this next chart? Every time your emotional switch is on, look at the steps below, and then come back to the chart above to choose the inner or outer skills or other values-based behaviors that are appropriate. And because we're data driven, it's important that you check the workability of these skills over and over. Remember, the workability of these skills is not about changing a feeling, getting rid of it, or pushing it down; the workability of using these skills and changing your behaviors is always in reference to your values.

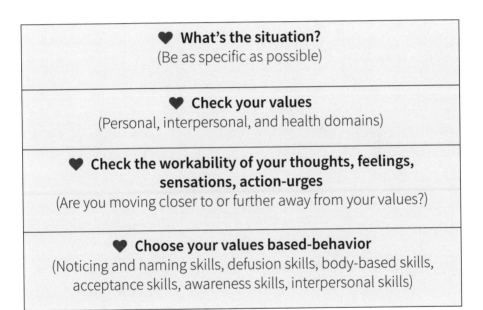

♥ **What's the situation?**
(Be as specific as possible)

♥ **Check your values**
(Personal, interpersonal, and health domains)

♥ **Check the workability of your thoughts, feelings, sensations, action-urges**
(Are you moving closer to or further away from your values?)

♥ **Choose your values based-behavior**
(Noticing and naming skills, defusion skills, body-based skills, acceptance skills, awareness skills, interpersonal skills)

TRY IT, TRACK IT, AND TRY IT AGAIN

When learning to dance, almost every new step, new movement, or new turn we learn begins with being stepped on, stepping on your partner's feet, stepping on your dress, or even getting a new bruise or a collection of them. The first time is the first time. The second time you try a new step it is a bit more comfortable. The third time you move more naturally, and on and on. The more you do it, the better it gets. The same applies to using these ACT skills in your daily life: the more you apply them, the better it gets when dealing with your emotional machinery. And because of the magic of the brain's plasticity, the more you use these ACT skills, the more you train your brain to get better and better at handling these emotional chains that come and go when your emotional switch is on.

I've learned that when trying new skills, all types of feelings show up in an emotional chain, like fear, concern, or distress, and they try to drag you with them; quickly your inner voice will try to make sense of them and come up with all types of thoughts for not getting out of your comfort zone and going back to old behaviors. Your inner voice is just doing its job and will quietly go into all types of modes. It may go into lawyer mode, listing 101 reasons for you not to try a new skill; it may possibly go into an authoritarian, bossy, or tyrannical voice, telling you not to do it. Or, it may go into a softy, best friendship-py voice, which may cutely ask you not to try something new. Are you going to respond to each one of those creations of your inner voice and spend hours explaining to it that you want to try a new behavior? Or can you pick up those thoughts, as if you're picking up little commentators in the radio news of your mind, and take them with you, along with those feelings of fear, concern, or anxiety, and do the doing that your values require of you?

Making a shift in your life comes with many moments of feeling awkward, weird, and out-of-sorts; the reality is that, no matter how skillful we are, or how many times we practice a skill, we all make mistakes from time to time (if you could see the laundry list of mistakes I have made in my life, you would be shocked). It's inevitable. When making mistakes, can you be compassionate toward yourself and defuse from thoughts such as "I'm too broken; nothing is going to make a difference; I'm a lost cause"? With curiosity and empathy, can you learn from those mistakes?

Every moment is a new moment to start.

Chapter 37: The Final Wrap-Up

Congratulations, you made it to the end! There are two last things I want to tell you: you're not broken and you're not alone. You're just wired to feel a lot. I hope you found this book helpful. I wrote it thinking of you, your hurts, struggles, and uniqueness as a human being. I deeply believe you deserve an amazing life and if you grabbed this book, you're still searching for it. I worked hard to put together applied skills from Acceptance and Commitment Therapy with the added benefits of affective science and the neurobiology of attachment.

Living your life as super-feeler is a process, not an outcome, and your success is not determined by doing exactly what the emotional machinery pushes you to do but by choosing how to live your life, every moment, and wherever you are, even if the emotions of the moment try to drag you down with them.

Moving forward, here is the key question you need to answer for yourself: when your emotional machinery gets triggered, are you willing to have those feelings, thoughts, memories, sensations, images, and go-to actions that come with it and still do what matters to you in that particular moment?

As the main character of the movie Battle of the Sexes said: "I'm done with talking; let's play." Here is my last sentence: less talking and more living for you!

With appreciation,

Dr. Z.

Appendix: Beyond the Scope of This Book

The purpose of this appendix is to give you some helpful tips on what to do about specific problematic situations that are beyond the scope of this book, such as chronic interpersonal problems, eating disorders, frequent para-suicidal and suicidal behaviors, medication and substance abuse, and trauma.

As you already know, as a super-feeler, you're wired to experience your emotions at a very intense level, as if you have an open wound; you feel anything and everything strongly, and a difficult situation is like salt added to the wound. From that place of vulnerability, you may find yourself struggling with an unstoppable chain of feelings moving at a fast speed; getting hooked on all those forecasting, labeling, ruling, retelling, and narrating thoughts; dealing with a body that may go into fight, flight, or freeze mode; getting stuck with painful memories from the past; and dwelling on those strong impulses to take action. Naturally, because the emotional machinery could drag you into a place of emotional misery, you come with all types of responses to handle your pain, such as overeating or undereating, thinking about suicide, engaging in self-harm behaviors, drinking, smoking marijuana, and abusing prescription medication. All of them are emotional management strategies.

What's the outcome of relying on those escapist responses? All of them work in the short term, but they're not sustainable in the long term. Sometimes these escapist responses take on a life of their own because they become overlearned behaviors, have a high frequency, and the more you rely on them, the more you teach your brain to search for them.

Let's go over these problematic situations that are beyond the scope of this book, with my recommendation on what you can do.

Chronic Interpersonal Problems

Do your relationships begin with positive moments, and then the negative ones come and outweigh the good moments? Do you go to gatherings and wonder how your friends have a laundry list of friends to count on? Relationships are complicated, and relationships in the life of a super-feeler can be a source of ongoing hurt, whether it's a friendship, dating relationship, or working relationship, to name a few. This book gave you the basics to create long-lasting and fulfilling relationships by identifying your interpersonal values, recognizing your relating/attachment styles, looking at your body language when communicating, practicing curious behaviors with others, distinguishing the go-to conflict tactics that you may rely on, and covering the basics of how to have a fair fight: practicing empathic and assertive behaviors. But even with all that, this is not a book solely focused on relationships.

If interpersonal problems are a chronic source of struggle in your life, then you need to augment your relationship skills. Here are two books I would recommend: *ACT with Love* by Russ Harris, M.D., and *ACT for Interpersonal Problems* by Matthew McKay, Ph.D., and Abigail Lev, Psy.D.

Eating Disorders

In chapter 2, you learned about some of the quick fixes that super-feelers rely on when their emotional switch is on: overeating, undereating, etc.

Here is a key point that I invite you to pay attention to: there is an important difference between using food-related behaviors to manage your hurts here and there versus fixating with white knuckles on how much or how little you eat, purging, using laxatives, jumping up and down in the bathroom between meals to manage your weight, counting how many grapes you eat, eating sparingly or skipping meals, worrying about eating a very healthy item to the point that if it doesn't feel safe you won't eat it, and more. All these latter examples are indicators that you could be struggling with an eating disorder that requires specialized treatment before it's fatal for your body and your life.

Here is the first step: get a medical checkup right away! Most physicians will order a blood test, electrolyte levels, vitamin D levels, and a thyroid panel to start. Your life matters, and as I tell my students over and over, it's better to practice prevention.

Para-Suicidal and Suicidal Behaviors

Feeling what you feel, with that much intensity, at that speed, and being drawn into action by overwhelming emotions, makes it very challenging to stop yourself from doing just about anything you can to get rid of your feelings, at any cost.

Sometimes you may use self-injury or self-harm behaviors to manage your hurts for all types of reasons: to relieve your pain, to let others know how much you're hurting, or to draw a line in the sand so that others don't do things that are upsetting to you, just to name a few reasons. You're certainly hurting and it's hard to be in your shoes. And yet, it's important to check in and ask yourself, what's the workability of those behaviors for you, your health, and your relationships? Are you getting closer to or further away from your personal values? There is no one better than you to check.

At other times, distressing feeling of hopelessness, discouragement, and gloominess push you to the point of desperation, and then your inner voice quickly comes up with a single solution to the struggle of going through this emotional chain — like death, suicide — to end this agony. You may have even researched the means to do it, written good-bye letters, chosen a date to commit suicide, or even shared with others your intentions. If you ever reached that point, even though I don't know you, I know you were hurting, and you were hurting so badly that your mind couldn't come up with any other solution than thinking about dying. Your inner voice was quickly problem solving with all the tools you had in that moment of struggle, and I get it: it's hard to be in your shoes. It's exhausting to have so much craving to be seen, respected, and loved, and be disappointed by life. And yet, in these instances, your inner voice is coming up with a single potential solution without looking at other tools, options, resources, people you have, or situations that may not be perfect but have brought value to your life at one point or another. Dear super-feeler, I am going to tell you only one thing in this moment: YOU MATTER!

It hurts to be in the middle of your struggle, and yet you can make a change with patience, dedication, and using the tools you learned in these chapters — not the tools that your emotions demand you use.

If you're at risk, have a plan, or you're on the edge of thinking about checking out, pause, and ask for specialized help right now. There is hope, there is work, and you make it happen.

Medication Abuse

Do you have an autoimmune disorder, back problems, or a chronic medical condition that causes you to be in constant pain? If you're dealing with a persistent, hard to change, and resistant medical condition, it's not easy to get through your day. You probably have to make all types of adjustments, from reorganizing your daily routine to how you interact with your body, how you stand up and sit down, your posture, the way you walk, and so on. It's hard to be in your shoes, and it's very time-consuming. You may have visited many doctors and gotten a long list of medications to take, from small ones to ones the size of your nail, and in all types of colors. It does make sense: you're physically hurting, your life is constantly affected by physical pain, and what's the quickest solution your inner voice comes up with? Take your pills.

Taking pills seems like a very reasonable step, except when your pain doesn't stop. And if your emotional machinery is activated, it really makes it very challenging to be in your shoes. Why wouldn't you keep taking medication if you're hurting so badly, and every time you take those pills there is a brief relief? Any human being would do what you have been doing. But here is the caveat. As good as it feels in the short term, you may be organizing your day, goals, and life around the pills. You may be moving along as long as there are pills around, and maybe now you're at the point where you cannot measure whether taking pills is a helper or a hook you're getting caught on. If you find yourself taking more of a medication than what was prescribed, it's important to step back and target this with your primary physician.

Substance Abuse

After Olivia, a super-feeler, lost her father in a car accident, she didn't know how to face her world without chatting with him every night; without realizing it, the two glasses of wine at night become a bottle while she recalled all types of memories with her dad: when he took her for a trip to Disneyland, when they baked that not-so-good chocolate cake in the kitchen, when she looked at him lying down in bed and he asked her to be his eyes when reading, or when they just watched

Saturday Night Live at home. In less than six months, Olivia found herself drinking secretly so no one would notice anything unusual; she managed to go to work and drop off her kids, and she just appeared to be sleepier than usual. Olivia knew that she was drinking throughout the day, some days more than others, and she didn't know how to stop. It all changed one day when she fell asleep with the stove on and the fire alarm went off.

Olivia was hurting after losing her father; he was the one person who knew her, cared for her, and had strong bonds with her. She did what she knew how to do: suppress, push down, and numb herself from all of the distressful and painful feelings. She didn't know better, didn't know any other skill. Every time she went into using a quick fix, she found herself struggling later with more loneliness, fears about getting fired, and embarrassment about doing something in secret, which made her feel ashamed. She was scared about her boyfriend finding out. She even felt lost about how to look after her children. She was in no position to remind them that abusing alcohol is not good for their health.

Substance abuse, whether it's beer, Scotch, wine, or vodka, can easily take on a life of its own without you realizing it, as it happens to many people. If you're a super-feeler and you're hurting and you find yourself quieting your pain with alcohol, ask yourself what the outcome of that behavior is in your life. There is no one better than you to check the workability of it.

If you find yourself drinking every day or are drinking more than two drinks each time, then you may be dealing with a substance abuse problem, and that is beyond the scope of this book. Ask for specialized help immediately. We have a limited amount of time on this earth, and every minute you're not living your values, that time is not coming back. You can always start right now, right here.

Trauma

Sometimes your life is disrupted and under threat because of an attack, a tragic accident, abuse, a natural disaster, war, or dozens of other situations that are not controllable. You get hurt and your mind brings nightmares, unwanted memories, and constant reminders about what happened to you. You avoid anything and everything related to what you went through. You may be constantly searching for threats and danger signals, and despite your efforts, you find yourself in a very uncomfortable place. For some people, their bodies go into a state of hyperarousal and they're on edge most of the time: your muscles are tense, and you visit cranky town most of the time. Other times, your body goes into hypo-arousal mode and your body actually checks out, numbs, and disconnects from the present moment. You go quickly into your internal world and you don't even realize that's happening. Those are forms of emotion regulation, and if you have experienced them for more than thirty days, then you may be dealing with posttraumatic stress disorder.

It's natural that when your emotional machinery is amplified, your inner voice and body are just trying to regulate what you experience to the best they can as independent systems, and at times it may feel like you're not in charge but the extra-overwhelming feelings associated with the traumatic event are.

As uncomfortable as it is, there is opportunity for you to overcome the impact of trauma in your life and have the life you deserve to have by practicing all the ACT skills you learned in these chapters. However, dealing with acute trauma reactions is beyond the scope of this book and you're going to require specialized help. Exposure therapy is a very well-researched trauma treatment with high efficacy. I recommend reading *Finding Life Beyond Trauma* by Victoria M. Follette, Ph.D., and Jacqueline Pistorello, Ph.D.

References

Bartsch, A., P. Vorderer, R. Mangold, and R. Viehoff. 2008. Appraisal of emotions in media use: Toward a process model of meta-emotion and emotion regulation. *Media Psychology* 11:7–27. doi:10.1080/15213260701813447

Cassidy, J., and P. R. Shaver. 2016. *Handbook of Attachment, 3rd Edition: Theory, Research, and Clinical Applications.* New York: Guilford Press.

Chapman, A. L., K. L. Gratz, and M. Z. Brown. 2006. Solving the puzzle of deliberate self-harm: The experiential avoidance model. *Behaviour Research and Therapy* 44:371–394. doi:10.1016/j.brat.2005.03.005

Craske, M. G., M. Treanor, C. C. Conway, T. Zbozinek, and B. Vervliet. 2014. Maximizing exposure therapy: An inhibitory learning approach. *Behaviour Research and Therapy* 58:10–23. doi:10.1016/j.brat.2014.04.006

Damasio, A. 2005. *Descartes' Error: Emotion, Reason, and the Human Brain.* New York: Penguin Books.

Dane, E., and M. G. Pratt. 2007. Exploring intuition and its role in managerial decision making. *Academy of Management Review* 32:33–54. doi:10.5465/amr.2007.23463682

Dane, E., K. W. Rockmann, and M. G. Pratt. 2012. When should I trust my gut? Linking domain expertise to intuitive decision-making effectiveness. *Organizational Behavior and Human Decision Processes* 119:187–194. doi:10.1016/j.obhdp.2012.07.009

Davidson, R. J., and S. Begley. 2012. *The Emotional Life of Your Brain: How Its Unique Patterns Affect the Way You Think, Feel, and Live—and How You Can Change Them.* New York: Avery.

Davies, C. D., A. N. Niles, A. Pittig, J. J. Arch, and M. G. Craske. 2015. Physiological and behavioral indices of emotion dysregulation as predictors of outcome from cognitive behavioral therapy and acceptance and commitment therapy for anxiety. *Journal of Behavior Therapy and Experimental Psychiatry* 46:35–43. doi:10.1016/j.jbtep.2014.08.002

Dewe, C., and R. Krawitz. 2007. Component analysis of dialectical behavior therapy skills training. *Australasian Psychiatry* 15:222–225. doi:10.1080/10398560701320345

Eisenberger, N. I., and M. D. Lieberman. 2004. Why rejection hurts: A common neural alarm system for physical and social pain. *Trends in Cognitive Sciences* 8:294–300. doi:10.1016/j.tics.2004.05.010

Follette, V. M., and J. Pistorello. 2007. *Finding Life Beyond Trauma*. Oakland, CA: New Harbinger.

Gilbert, P. 2009. Introducing compassion-focused therapy. *Advances in Psychiatric Treatment* 15:199–208. doi:10.1192/apt.bp.107.005264

Gladwell, M. 2002. *The Tipping Point: How Little Things Can Make a Difference*. New York: Back Bay Books.

Glenn, C. R., and E. D. Klonsky. 2009. Emotion dysregulation as a core feature of borderline personality disorder. *Journal of Personality Disorders* 23:20–28.

Gloster, A. T., J. Klotsche, J. Ciarrochi, G. Eifert, R. Sonntag, H. Wittchen, and J. Hoyer. 2017. Increasing valued behaviors precedes reduction in suffering: Findings from a randomized controlled trial using ACT. *Behaviour Research and Therapy* 91:64–71. doi:10.1016/j.brat.2017.01.013

Goleman, D. 1995. *Emotional Intelligence*. New York: Bantam Books.

Gottman, J., and N. Silver. 2007. *The Seven Principles for Making Marriage Work*. New York: Harmony, 2015.

Gratz, K. L., and J. G. Gunderson. 2006. Preliminary data on an acceptance-based emotion regulation group intervention for deliberate self-harm among women with borderline personality disorder. *Behavior Therapy* 37:25–35. doi:10.1016/j.beth.2005.03.002

Gyurak, A., J. J. Gross, and A. Etkin. 2011. Explicit and implicit emotion regulation: A dual-process framework. *Cognition and Emotion* 25:400–412. http://proxy.wi.edu:2083/10.1080/02699931.2010.544160

Haidt, J. 2003. The moral emotions. In *Handbook of Affective Sciences*, ed. R. J. Davidson, K. R. Scherer, and H. H. Goldsmith, 852–870. Oxford: Oxford University Press.

Harned, M. S., K. E. Korslund, and M. M. Linehan. 2014. A pilot randomized controlled trial of Dialectical Behavior Therapy with and without the Dialectical Behavior Therapy Prolonged Exposure protocol for suicidal and self-injuring women with borderline personality disorder and PTSD. *Behaviour Research and Therapy* 55:7–17. doi:10.1016/j.brat.2014.01.008

Hayes, S. C., K. D. Strosahl, and K. G. Wilson. 2016. *Acceptance and Commitment Therapy: The Process and Practice of Mindful Change*. 2nd ed. New York: Guilford Press.

Hulbert-Williams, L., K. Hochard, N. Hubert-Williams, R. Archer, W. Nicholls, and K. Wilson. 2016. Contextual behavioural coaching: An evidence-based model for supporting behaviour change. *International Coaching Psychology Review* 11:142–150.

Izard, C. E. 2009. Emotion theory and research: Highlights, unanswered questions, and emerging issues. *Annual Review of Psychology* 60:1–25. doi:10.1146/annurev.psych.60.110707.163539

Kahneman, D., and G. Klein. 2009. Conditions for intuitive expertise: A failure to disagree. *American Psychologist* 64:515–526. doi:10.1037/a0016755

Kahneman, D., P. Slovic, and A. Tversky. 1982. *Judgment Under Uncertainty: Heuristics and Biases.* Cambridge, UK: Cambridge University Press.

Kashdan, T. B., L. F. Barrett, and P. E. McKnight. 2015. Unpacking emotion differentiation: Transforming unpleasant experience by perceiving distinctions in negativity. *Current Directions in Psychological Science* 24:10–16. doi:http://proxy.wi.edu:2083/10.1177/0963721414550708

Kashdan, T. B., and A. S. Farmer. 2014. Differentiating emotions across contexts: Comparing adults with and without social anxiety disorder using random, social interaction, and daily experience sampling. *Emotion* 14:629–638. http://proxy.wi.edu:2083/10.1037/a0035796

Leahy, R. L. 2012. Emotional schema therapy: A bridge over troubled waters. In *Acceptance and Mindfulness in Cognitive Behavior Therapy*, ed. J. D. Herbert and E. M. Forman, 109–131. Marblehead, MA: John Wiley & Sons. doi:10.1002/9781118001851.ch5

Linehan, M. M., K. E. Korslund, M. S. Harned, R. J. Gallop, A. Lungu, A. D. Neacsiu, J. McDavid, et al. 2015. Dialectical behavior therapy for high suicide risk in individuals with borderline personality disorder. *JAMA Psychiatry* 72:475–482. doi:10.1001/jamapsychiatry.2014.3039

Luoma, J. B., and J. L. Villatte. 2012. Mindfulness in the treatment of suicidal individuals. *Cognitive and Behavioral Practice* 19:265–276. doi:10.1016/j.cbpra.2010.12.003

Lynch, T. R., R. J. Hempel, and C. Dunkley. 2015. Radically Open-Dialectical Behavior Therapy for disorders of over-control: Signaling matters. *American Journal of Pyschotherapy* 69:141–159.

Mauss, I. B., A. J. Shallcross, A. S. Troy, O. P. John, E. Ferrer, F. H. Wilhelm, and J. J. Gross. 2011. Don't hide your happiness! Positive emotion dissociation, social connectedness, and psychological functioning. *Journal of Personality and Social Psychology* 100:738–748. doi:10.1037/a0022410

Morton, J., S. Snowdon, M. Gopold, and E. Guymer. 2012. Acceptance and Commitment Therapy group treatment for symptoms of borderline personality disorder: A public sector pilot study. *Cognitive and Behavioral Practice* 19:527–544. doi:10.1016/j.cbpra.2012.03.005

Nyberg, F. 2014. Structural plasticity of the brain to psychostimulant use. *Neuropharmacology* 87:115–124. doi:10.1016/j.neuropharm.2014.07.004

Schulze, L., C. Schmahl, and I. Niedtfeld. 2016. Neural correlates of disturbed emotion processing in borderline personality disorder: A multimodal meta-analysis. *Biological Psychiatry* 79:97–106. http://proxy.wi.edu:2083/10.1016/j.biopsych.2015.03.027

Siegel, D. J. 1999. *The Developing Mind: Toward a Neurobiology of Interpersonal Experience.* New York: Guilford Press.

———. 2010. *The Mindful Therapist: A Clinician's Guide to Mindsight and Neural Integration* (Norton Series on Interpersonal Neurobiology). New York: W. W. Norton & Company.

Smith, N. K., J. T. Larsen, T. L. Chartrand, J. T. Cacioppo, H. A. Katafiasz, and K. E. Moran. 2006. Being bad isn't always good: Affective context moderates the attention bias toward negative information. *Journal of Personality and Social Psychology* 90:210–220. doi:10.1037/0022-3514.90.2.210

Todd, R. M., W. A. Cunningham, A. K. Anderson, and E. Thompson. 2012. Affect-biased attention as emotion regulation. *Trends in Cognitive Sciences* 16:365–372. http://proxy.wi.edu:2083/10.1016/j.tics.2012.06.003

Tavris, C. 1989. *Anger: The Misunderstood Emotion*. Rev. ed. New York: Simon and Schuster.

Wilks, C. R., K. E. Korslund, M. S. Harned, and M. M. Linehan. 2016. Dialectical behavior therapy and domains of functioning over two years. *Behaviour Research and Therapy* 77:162–169. doi:10.1016/j.brat.2015.12.013

Index